THE BABY BOOMERS' COOKBOOK

Helen Townsend

SIMON & SCHUSTER

AUSTRALIA

THE BABY BOOMERS' COOKBOOK

First published in Australasia in 1991 by
Simon & Schuster Australia
20 Barcoo Street, East Roseville NSW 2069

A Paramount Communications Company
Sydney New York London Toronto Tokyo Singapore

© 1991 Helen Townsend

National Library of Australia
Cataloguing in Publication data

Townsend, Helen.
   Baby boomers cookbook.

   Includes index.
   ISBN 0 7318 0217 9.

   1. Cookery, Australian. I. Title.

641.5994
Designed by Kathie Baxter Smith/Design Smiths
Typeset in Australia by Adtype Graphics Pty Ltd
Printed in Singapore by Toppan Printing Co.

CONTENTS

Want special recipes?
...Hints?
..Advice?

THERE ARE recipes for every occasion between these covers.
Delicious suggestions that fill out your reputation as a cook.
But should you need a recipe for a special occasion and you can't
find it in this Recipe Book; if you'd like particular cooking
information or hints; if something goes wrong with any recipe
you try, write to me at The Betty King Kitchen. Address your
query to Betty King, Box 2625, G.P.O., Sydney, and we will
be happy to supply the necessary recipe or information promptly.

For now, kindest regards and good cooking, from

Betty King

Senior Home Economist
World Brands Pty. Ltd.

Baby Boomers and Their Tucker

Father is the butcher,
Mother cuts the meat,
I'm the little frankfurt,
That runs around the street.

Remember the brown bits on the roast, the crust on the apple pie, the smell of Anzac biscuits, the texture of passionfruit flummery? If you do, chances are you're a baby boomer. Chances are that you also remember the horrors of baby boomer food — stewed neck chops, boiled tripe, overcooked vegetables and stale sponge.

The baby boomers have turned the tables on the tucker they were raised on. We rejected the food of our childhood, embraced cheap red wine with a vengeance and dined on the foreign food that our parents regarded as — well, foreign. We rejected the full cream milk and lashings of butter we were brought up on. We rejected the sacred notion that you have to eat meat once a day. We decided we didn't need three-course breakfasts or pudding every night. In the process we became healthier and thinner.

In our scramble for brown rice, cuisine minceur and the Pritikin wisdom, we forgot one thing. We forgot just how terrific some of the food we had as children actually was.

When I wrote the book *Baby Boomers*, I gathered my material in a series of dinner parties. To kick-start the guests' memories, I served food that neither I nor my guests had eaten since childhood — steak and kidney pudding, home-made apple pie, mulligatawny soup, lemon delicious, Welsh rarebit, roast lamb and rabbit pie. Not only did this have the desired effect of taking us back to the days of Globite suitcases and God Save the Queen, but we all felt a strange satisfaction with the food. We made fun of boiled sausages and fried scones but — almost shamefaced — we realised that much of the food of the baby boomer era, was in fact, terrific.

That's what this book is all about. Good, basic, honest, home-cooked food. I've included the very best of some wonderful meat recipes, the extraordinary puddings, the cakes and bikkies that seemed at times to be the mainstay of the baby boomer diet. Our mothers were economy-minded and there are some great meals that use up left-overs, some delicious soups and, for the truly nostalgic, some lollies. I haven't included the recipe for toad-in-a-hole or curried cold meat or anything else I don't like.

Some of the recipes I have modified a little. The meat is a little rarer, there is less fat and sugar, and I've used short-cuts where appropriate. I have compiled the recipes more in accordance with the spirit of baby boomer times than with a concern for absolute authenticity.

Collecting the recipes was an interesting process. My first step was to raid my mother's recipe files — a collection of faded and stained newspaper cuttings, handwritten recipes on scraps of paper, cards that used to come with packets of flour, recipes peeled off tins of baking powder or snipped from boxes of cocoa. Other women of the same era had remarkably similar collections.

Looking through these was fascinating. They conjured up the community network that was such an important part of the baby boomer childhood. Women wrote out recipes for each other, scribbled comments on them — *use less ginger!* — exchanged cookbooks and "lent" each other ingredients. As a child, I was sent next-door to borrow a cup of sugar, and I remember the neighbours coming to our back door to ask for an egg for the cake. Nowadays, we don't send our kids next-door. The neighbours probably aren't home and anyway, we're in the habit of driving up to the local supermarket.

Recipe books have changed too. The ones I collected were a wonderful reflection of the era. There seemed to be a recipe book for every religion. The Presbyterians, in particular, seemed ardent publishers of cookbooks. Organisations like the Country Women's Association did very nicely out of cookbooks. Others were written by domestic science mistresses or issued by local progress associations. Judging by the numbers of editions, there was an insatiable demand.

These cookbooks were densely printed, with few illustrations. Improvisation in the kitchen (or even having a good time) was not encouraged. It was as important to be able to beat your sponge for half an hour as it was to set your table properly. The books were full of warnings — *stand on a rubber mat while ironing*, and potions — *remedy for beesting*. Most books had a section on invalid cooking. The dishes were enough to make even the hale and hearty turn their face to the wall. They also shed light on why we baby boomers may be a little neurotic about food. The chapters on children's cookery indicate that, as babies, we were force-fed on a mixture of custard, mixed vegetables, mashed brains and junket.

Despite all this, the 1940s, 50s and 60s was an exciting era in the kitchen. After the war, new kerosene fridges and stoves replaced ice-chests and safes. These soon gave way to electric and gas appliances. There were modern convenience products like margarine in tubs, packet pastry and — later — frozen peas. The 60s brought us

Date Pudding
1 cup S R Flour
1 " Bread crumbs
1 " Dates
½ Sultanas (not necessary)
½ teaspoon nutmeg (small)
½ " cinnamon (")
1 small cup sugar
2 oz Butter or marg.
½ teaspoonful soda dissolved in a little milk ¼ Pint
1 large or 2 small eggs
cream butter sugar add egg then other ingredients
if mixture seem to stiff add a little milk
Steam for 2 hrs

the excitement of gadgets — electric mixers, electric jaffle irons, toasters that popped the toast up before your very eyes. Blenders and primitive food processors made their appearance.

The kitchen itself changed from the scrubbed wood benches with a marble pastry board and lino on the floor to an all-modern, all-electric, vinyl and laminex dream. Feature walls and multi-coloured cupboards sometimes gave these modern kitchens a nightmare quality. But people loved it all, along with new gadgets like pegboards

and knife-racks and multi-coloured, mail-order plastic containers in sets of four.

The real change came at the beginning of the 70s, at the end of our baby boomer childhood. We became more cosmopolitan. Magazines included specials on Asian cooking and cardamom and coriander appeared on the spice-racks next to the old favourites of cinnamon, nutmeg and allspice. Herbs no longer meant just the parsley and mint that grew on the sides of the vegie patch. Australia — land of milk, honey, meat and two veg — was finally expanding its culinary horizons.

There's no way we could go back to the cuisine of the post-war era. But there's every reason for enjoying the very best of it. For those of us who grew up then, the recipes in this book will offer a nostalgia component as well as a good feed. For those who had the misfortune not to be baby boomers, I hope this book will open up new food horizons.

Baby boomer way to start the day

Baby boomers grew up in the era before the ensuite bathroom. Our post-war fifties homes proudly boasted an *inside* bathroom, but it was shared by everyone. In the morning rush, Dad shaved there, Mum showered, the kids washed their hands before breakfast. We were told not to dirty the sink, spill the tooth powder or leave the tap running. In big families, there was always a queue outside the door.

Getting dressed for school was more complicated than it is today. There was a military air to it. We wore lace-up leather shoes which had to be polished. Girls in high schools wore stockings and suspenders. If you lost the little rubber bit, you used a sixpence to keep your stocking up. Everybody wore ties and some posh schools insisted on hats, and gloves for girls.

The military influence spread to the kitchen where Mum was rather like an army cook dishing up daily rations. The cooked breakfast we baby boomers had served up every morning was a formidable meal. There was a pot of porridge on the stove, a box of cornflakes on the table. You sliced a banana over your cornflakes, added milk and sugar and fought with your brother over who got the collector's card at the bottom of the pack. There were all sorts of devious ways of getting hold of the card before you finished the box.

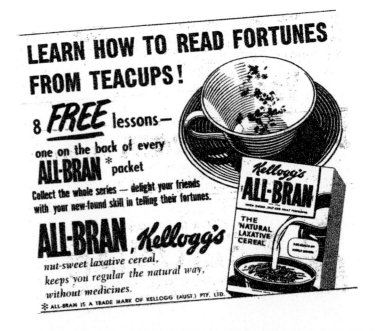

FOOD AND ITS FUNCTIONS

Foods are divided into three classes:

1. Flesh Forming Foods are the Proteins which contain a lot of nitrogen. These are essential to good health, and an adult requires $4\frac{1}{2}$ ounces per day.

We get them from all meats, fish, eggs, milk, cheese, peas, beans, lentils, flour.

2. Heat and Energy Producers are the starches and sugars. An adult requires 14 ounces per day. They are found in all grains, cereals, potatoes, fruits, sugarcane, beetroot, milk, etc. Fats produce heat in the body, and an adult requires $2\frac{1}{2}$ ounces per day. They are found in butter, suet, dripping, milk, oils from nuts and fish.

3. Blood Purifiers and Bone Makers are the mineral salts, vitamins and water. An adult requires 1 ounce per day of mineral salts. They are found in all fruits and vegetables, water, and milk. Vitamins are found in all fresh fruit and vegetables as well as in fresh milk, fresh eggs, fresh butter, cod liver oil, marmite, etc.

Breakfast was a pretty riotous meal. Mum was busy at the stove and Dad seldom wanted to have much to do with the kids at that hour. "She took my bacon . . . he ate all the toast . . . he's feeding the dog under the table." Guerrilla war at 7 a.m.

Some mothers squeezed orange juice, and if you were upmarket you had sour grapefruit, served with those special pointy grapefruit spoons. There was a pot of tea, a jug of milk and bowl of sugar on the table. That was just for starters.

Then there were boiled eggs, poached eggs, fried eggs, scrambled eggs or coddled eggs. To go with the eggs, there were fried tomatoes, bottled from last season's crop, baked beans and bacon. Sausages were part of the meal, and if you lived in the country, there were often a couple of chops as well.

All this came with toast, with lots of butter. There was more toast after that, to eat with jam or Lackerstein's marmalade. Often, the jam was home-made, reflecting the gluts of various fruits during the previous year. It was bottled in last year's peanut butter jars, with waxed paper over the top, and always labelled with the date and the variety. We always avoided Aunty Jo's choko jam. It had chokoes in it and we didn't eat those on principle.

The toast kept coming. The bread delivered by the baker was unsliced, so Mum was hard at work slicing it, then putting it into the toaster. Black smoke heralded disaster and sometimes elicited a less than ladylike response from the cook.

BABY BOOMER WAY TO START THE DAY

The person who invented the pop-up toaster was a genius. The old-style toaster had two doors that you had to keep opening to check how things were going. Then it had to be turned. From memory, there seemed a fairly high risk of getting your fingers burnt or of being electrocuted.

There were, occasionally, special breakfast dishes, perhaps fried kidneys once a week, or eggs and anchovy, a dish I remember with scant affection. Pork sausages were supposed to be a real treat, but I remember them as being much the same as any other sort of sausage. Brains in egg and breadcrumbs and scalloped eggs were not served every day. We got mushrooms on toast if we had been mushroom-picking in the country the day before. Omelettes were a rarity because of their tendency to go leathery. If Mum added shallots, chances were you scored a French omelette.

It's a wonder we could think, let alone walk after consuming such a meal.

Dad was first out of the house, in his work clothes and always with a hat on. Dads didn't go anywhere without their hats.

Children had to undergo inspection before leaving the house. "Are your fingernails clean? Have you got a hanky? Did you polish your shoes? Have you got your lunch? The drink out of the freezer? Don't let Johnny catch a bus on his own."

Our mothers must have breathed a sigh of relief once we had all gone, but she was left with an enormous number of dirty dishes and pots and pans and a day's housework ahead.

I'm not certain when families stopped having those stupendous breakfasts and I'm not sure what stopped us. Maybe our poor mothers just ran out of energy. Maybe it occurred to somebody that the relatively sedentary twentieth century family didn't require an enormous protein, fat, carbohydrate kick-start at the beginning of each day.

However, traces of the baby boomer breakfast still linger. The same breakfast cereals that sold then are still the most popular. The porridge may be instant, but we still eat it. Bacon may not be good for your cholesterol levels, but it's the best thing with a fried egg. And personally, I can't start the day without a slice of Vegemite toast and a cup of tea.

1 THE SUNDAY ROAST AND OTHER GREAT MEAT AND FISH DISHES

Mary had a little lamb,
Then she had some more.
After fifty helpings,
She fell down on the floor.

The conscientious baby boomer mother insisted that children eat meat at least once a day. The theory was that if a little meat was good for you, a lot would ensure you really did grow up straight and strong. Mothers were also concerned with *economy* which meant that some of the meat dishes were truly frightful. But despite the horrors, there were some wonderful, succulent, tasty (even truly economical!) meals.

CUTS OF MUTTON SUITABLE FOR
Baking: 1. Leg; 6. Shoulder; 2. Loin. Boiling: 1. Leg; 5b. Neck; Sheeps' tongues; 7. Corned breast; 9. Shanks; 10. Trotters. Grilling: 2. Short Loin Chops; 3. Chump Chops; 4. Cutlets. Stewing: 7. Breast; 5b. Neck chops; Brains; Kidneys. Soups: Head; 9. Shanks; 5a. Neck.

ROAST LEG OF LAMB

Sunday roast was the culinary triumph of the baby boomer era. The gravy, the brown bits on the meat, the cauliflower, the baked potatoes and parsnips, the Yorkshire pudding, all went to make up that delicious weekly event. The lawn had been mown, the kids had been to Sunday school and all was right with the world. The Sunday roast drew the family together. You might have to pay for it with cold meat on Monday, curry on Tuesday, and cold meat sandwiches at school, but to most baby boomers it was worth it.

The meat

Method

When buying the leg, make sure you know the weight of it, as this determines cooking time. Allow 20 minutes per 500 g (1 lb). This means that the outside of the lamb will be brown, but the inside will still be slightly pink. (This is an adjustment for modern palates. Meat used to be roasted to death, with at least 30 minutes per 500 g (1 lb).)

Allow the oven to heat to 250°C (500°F). Put the roast in the baking dish with about half a cup of water. This will stop it from sticking. If you are going to cook Yorkshire pudding to go with it, put the roast on a rack.

When the roast has been in the oven for 20 minutes, reduce the heat to 200°C (400°F). After this, it requires very little attention. All you need to do is take a look at it to make sure it is cooking but not burning. You can tell when it is cooked when you prick it with a skewer: if the juice that comes out of it is clear, it's ready.

The vegies

For the boomer roast dinner, there are two types of vegetables — those cooked with the meat and those cooked separately. Potatoes, pumpkin, parsnips and onions are cooked with the roast. As you peel these, try to keep each type approximately the same size. Otherwise, some will be undercooked and others overcooked. Potatoes and onions usually take about 45 minutes. Pumpkin and parsnips usually take 30 minutes at 200°C (400°F).

TIME-TABLE FOR COOKING MEATS

BEEF AND MUTTON—
15 minutes to each pound and 15 minutes over.
MEAT WITHOUT BONE—
20 minutes to each pound and 20 minutes over.
PORK AND VEAL—
25 minutes to each pound and 20 minutes over.
CORNED ROUND—
25 minutes to each pound and 25 minutes over.
CORNED BRISKET—
30 minutes to each pound and 30 minutes over.
PICKLED PORK—
25 minutes to each pound and 25 minutes over.
HAM—25 minutes to each pound and 25 minutes over.
TONGUE—Two to three hours, according to size.

Yorkshire pudding

If you are making Yorkshire pudding, cook the vegetables separately in another pan. Roast the meat on a rack and cook the Yorkshire pudding with it, in the same roasting pan, for the last 20 minutes.

Ingredients

120 g (4 oz) plain flour
1 egg yolk
200 mL (8 fl oz) milk
salt

Method

Mix the ingredients together and beat well. Make sure there is enough fat in the roasting pan. If it is very dry, add a few spoonfuls of oil. Give it time to heat and spread and then pour in the batter. It will cook in 20–30 minutes at 200°C (400°F).

The gravy

Blend a tablespoon of plain flour into the pan juices. Heat gently on the top of the stove, stirring all the time, gradually adding water to form gravy. Baby boomer mothers used to add Bovril or Gravox to make sure the gravy was brown. The modern alternative is a dash of soy.

Mint sauce

Chop finely 6 mint leaves. Add 2 tablespoons of white sugar. Add a little boiling water to dissolve the sugar. Add 2 tablespoons of vinegar and allow to stand for 15 minutes before serving.

POT ROAST

The wonderful thing about a pot roast is the way it makes the kitchen smell — a mouth-watering aroma of meat and vegies cooking in the most wonderful way possible. Try it! The end result is as good as it smells.

A rolled roast is often the best for this method of cooking. Cheaper cuts are okay as this method of cooking makes the meat tender, but make sure the roast is not too fatty.

Method

Melt 2 tablespoons of dripping (or oil) in a large saucepan. The saucepan should be a fair bit bigger than the meat as later you will need room to add the vegetables. Brown the meat on all sides. Turn down the heat to low, put the lid on the saucepan and cook for 1 hour. Prepare potatoes, onions and pumpkin. Take the meat out, turn up the heat and brown the vegetables. Put the meat back in, turn down the heat again and cook for another hour. A piece of meat over 1.5 kg (3 lb) will need cooking for an extra 30 minutes in the first stage.

Remove meat and vegetables. Skim fat from the liquid in the pot. Blend some flour and water and add to the juices in the pot to make gravy. A dash of red wine at this stage does not go astray.

This dish can be cooked in a pressure-cooker, after taking the same preliminary steps. If the meat is frozen, it will need about 30 minutes per 500 g (1 lb) on high pressure. If it is not frozen, it will need about 40 minutes per kilo (2 lb). In a pressure-cooker, the vegetables take about 4 minutes on high pressure.

Cowardy, cowardy custard,
Made to eat your mustard,
Mustard hot, spat the lot,
Cowardy, cowardy custard.

See you later,
Hot potato.

Steak and kidney pudding

A lot of people who disliked this dish as children develop a real love of it as adults. Granted, suet isn't the most attractive ingredient, but get the butcher to shred it and you'll soon overcome any aversion to it. Suet crust, with this wonderful gravy and meat, is all you need on a cold winter's night.

Ingredients

700 g (1 lb 4 oz) blade or round steak

3 lamb's kidneys

2 onions

1 dessertspoon plain flour

water

salt

coarse black pepper

The pastry crust

180 g (6 oz) plain flour

½ teaspoon baking powder

1 pinch salt

90 g (3 oz) suet

iced water

Serves 6

Method

Cut up the steak into 2.5 cm (1 in) cubes. Skin the kidneys and chop into 1 cm (½ in) pieces. Brown in a non-stick pan. Add coarsely cut onions and allow them to brown. Sprinkle with flour and allow it to soak into the meat juices. Gradually, on a low heat, add water to make gravy. There should be just enough liquid to cover the meat and onions. Season with salt and plenty of coarse black pepper. Simmer gently.

For the pastry, put flour, baking powder and salt in a bowl and mix well. Remove membrane and red pieces from the suet before shredding it on a cheese grater. Rub the suet into the flour mixture and then add enough iced water to make a stiff paste. Knead lightly on a floured board. Put aside a third of the pastry for the crust. Roll out the larger piece into a round shape about 6 mm (¼ in) thick. Grease a pudding basin and fit the crust into it. Trim if needed, leaving a little above the rim.

Fill the basin with the meat mixture. Roll out the remaining crust to fit the top, put it on and pinch both pastry edges together around the sides. Tie on a pudding cloth or lid. Cook in boiling water for 3 hours, or pressure-cook for 45 minutes on low pressure. If cooking

Two little sausages, in the
  frying pan,
One went pop, the other
  went bang.

in a saucepan, check the water level during cooking and add more water as needed.

In theory, the pudding can be turned out of the basin, but it may collapse. For first attempts, serve at the table, with a large white serviette wrapped around the basin.

Shepherd's Pie

There are numerous versions of this dish, depending on how economy-minded you are. The worst I ever tasted was some gristly bits of cold meat soaked in Worcester and tomato sauce, with some mashed potato on top.

The best, given below, is a wonderful and simple dish. It is also economical and can be reheated if it survives more than one meal.

Ingredients

500 g (1 lb) lean mince

2 onions

1½ tablespoons flour

1 × 400 g (12 oz) can tomatoes

4 large potatoes

butter and milk for mashing the potato

salt

Serves 6

Method

Chop the onions coarsely, then brown them with a little of the mince. Gradually add more mince, browning it as you go. Sprinkle the flour over the mixture and then add the tomatoes to make the gravy. Stir the mixture, breaking up the tomatoes, and cook until any excess liquid has been reduced — the mixture should be moist, but not runny. Place into a pie dish.

Peel the potatoes and then boil or microwave them until they are soft. Mash them well with milk, a little butter and salt to season. They should be slightly more moist than mashed potatoes served straight onto the plate. Cover the meat mixture with the mashed potato. Bake in a moderate oven until the top is slightly browned. Serve with tomato sauce.

God Save our gracious cat,
Feed her on bread and fat.
God save the cat.

MEAT PIE

This dish is not related to the traditional Aussie meat pie eaten at football matches and other events of national importance. This is a main meal. Any leftovers will be preyed upon by phantom midnight snackers.

Ingredients

1 kg (2.2 lb) steak (round or skirt are the best cuts)

2 onions

1 tablespoon plain flour

200 ml (7 fl oz) water

salt and black pepper

2 large carrots

2 medium potatoes

Flaky pastry (use frozen pastry if you prefer)

250 g (8 oz) plain flour

½ teaspoon baking powder

1 pinch salt

½ cup water

125 g (4 oz) butter

milk or egg yolk to glaze

Serves 6

Method

Cut up the meat into generous, bite-size chunks and brown in a saucepan. Add the onions and allow to brown. Add the flour, blend and then add the water to make gravy. Add the salt and pepper. Simmer for an hour or until meat is tender. Cut the carrots into slices and add to the mixture while it is still hot. Boil the potatoes in a separate saucepan for about 15 minutes, or until they are still firm and not completely cooked. Cut into slices and put aside.

While the meat mixture is cooling, make the pastry. Mix the dry ingredients thoroughly. Add enough of the water to form a soft dough. Roll into a ball and then roll out a third of the dough onto a floured board. Spread with a third of the butter, making sure to keep it away from the edges. Dredge a little flour over it and then fold into three. Roll out again, add another third of the butter and repeat the procedure. Add the final third of the butter in the same way and then roll out till the dough is slightly larger than the pie dish, with enough over to form a crust around the edge.

Place the meat mixture into the pie dish. Lay the slices of potato over the top. Put an egg-cup (beware of plastic) in the centre so the pie doesn't collapse. Form a pastry crust around the edge. Put on the pastry lid, pinching its edges together with the crust. From pastry leftovers cut some leaf shapes for decoration. Make some small holes to allow steam to escape, glaze with milk or egg yolk, and bake in a hot oven until golden brown.

CORNED BEEF

Serve hot with parsley sauce, or cold with mustard. As a child, corned beef seemed to go on forever — hot corned beef, cold corned beef cold corned beef again, corned beef sandwiches, corned beef on toast, corned beef hash. As a result of this oversupply in years gone by, until recently I only ever bought corned beef by the slice from the deli. However, I found that butchers now sell it in smaller pieces, and cooking your own not only allows you to enjoy it hot, but also produces corned beef of a superior texture and flavour.

Ingredients

1 piece of corned beef (silverside has less fat than the rolled variety)

10 peppercorns

6 cloves

1 bay leaf

1 onion

The sauce

1 tablespoon butter

1 tablespoon plain flour

250 ml (8 fl oz) milk

a bunch of parsley

Method

When you buy the meat, make sure you ask the butcher how much the piece weighs.

Put the meat in a large pot, cover it with water and add peppercorns, cloves, bay leaf and onion. Bring to the boil and simmer gently, allowing 1 hour for every kilo (2.2 lb) of meat. If you use a pressure-cooker, cook in the same way, but allow 15 minutes on high per 500 g (1 lb), with a minimum of 20 minutes for any piece. If the piece is long and thin, it will need less time than a thick piece.

Make up the white sauce by melting the butter, blending in the flour, adding the milk and bringing gently to the boil. Chop parsley finely and add to the sauce.

Cut the meat in thin slices and spoon a little of the white sauce over the meat. Serve with potato fritters (see page 84) and a green vegetable.

IRISH STEW

I have no memories of eating this dish as a child, and I took this to be a bad sign until I had it cooked for me by an enthused baby boomer cook and became an instant convert. It is surprisingly delicate and subtle in flavour.

Ingredients

500 g (1 lb) lamb neck chops

30 g (1 oz) plain flour

salt

black pepper

500 ml (16 fl oz) water

1 bay leaf

2 onions

4 potatoes

1 tablespoon chopped parsley

Serves 4–6

Method

Remove gristle and fat from the chops. Mix the flour, salt and pepper and dip each chop into the mixture. Put the chops into a saucepan and add water so they are just covered. Stir in the remaining flour, then add the remaining water and the bay leaf. Simmer for 45 minutes. Chop the onions and potatoes and place them on top of the meat. Simmer gently for another hour. Serve with a liberal sprinkling of parsley.

This is another excellent pressure-cooker dish. Cook on high pressure for 15 minutes.

The butcher, the baker, the
candlestick maker,
They all jumped out of a
rotten potato.

BEEF STEW WITH SUET DUMPLINGS

Another great dish from the Irish!

Ingredients

500 g (1 lb) round steak or blade

2 onions

2 tablespoons plain flour

1 cup water

1 beef stock cube

The dumplings

180 g (6 oz) flour

½ teaspoon baking powder

1 pinch salt

90 g (3 oz) suet

½ cup water

Serves 6

Method

Cut the meat into cubes and brown in a frypan with the chopped onions. Sprinkle some flour over the meat and onions, and add water and stock cube to make a rich brown gravy. There should be more gravy than in an ordinary casserole or stew. Combine the remaining flour, salt and baking powder in a bowl and rub in the finely chopped suet. Add water slowly to form a stiff dough. Cut into 8 pieces and roll each into a ball. Add to the stew which can be cooked either as a casserole in a slow oven or on top of the stove at a gentle heat. Cook for 1 hour.

A FEW CATERING HINTS

One 2 lb. sandwich loaf will cut approximately 60 small sandwiches.

A ½ lb. butter is sufficient to spread a 2 lb. loaf for sandwiches.

One lb. sugar is sufficient for 100 people.

Three pints of milk is sufficient for tea for 50 people.

A gallon of milk is sufficient for 50 cups of coffee.

THE DRIPPING DISH AND OTHER FAT STORIES

I had not thought of dripping for years. I had forgotten the rituals which accompanied the collection of dripping, the bowl of dripping that stood by the stove, the jars of dripping in the fridge. I am glad I had forgotten dripping and I hope I will forget it again. However, a baby boomers' cookbook would not be complete without a mention of dripping.

Early baby boomers remember collecting dripping to feed the poor starving Brits at the end of the war. They took it to school in old jamjars to be shipped off across the oceans. Later, when the Poms came here, they told us about our rancid dripping arriving in ships from Australia. They certainly didn't want to eat it, so they either threw it down the drain or made it into soap. So much for international goodwill.

You could actually buy dripping at the butcher's, but most people simply collected the fat off a cooked roast and put it in a bowl. The brown bits went to the bottom and the top layers were sort of yellowy. Some people went through some strange ritual to clarify the dripping, so it could be used to make cakes and biscuits. Most people simply re-used it for frying, for roasting, or on bread instead of butter. I remember my grandmother relished the brown bits at the bottom of the dripping bowl on a slice of fresh white bread.

We never used it on bread, but it was always there, by the stove. On hot days it would begin to melt, with an oily film over the top. On cold days it would be white and solid. As I said, I hope I will forget about dripping.

Butter was considered to be a health food and we were encouraged to spread it thickly on our white bread. Well, not too thickly, because it was expensive. But we were the land of milk and honey and butter, so it was readily available. You also used butter in the best cakes, like the ones for special afternoon tea or the Christmas cake, so it would keep well.

Compared to the modern product, baby boomer margarine was revolting. It came in blocks, wrapped in paper, and it came off the block in splinters and tasted something like sump oil.

Well, that may be a slight exaggeration but we knew why they said butter was better.

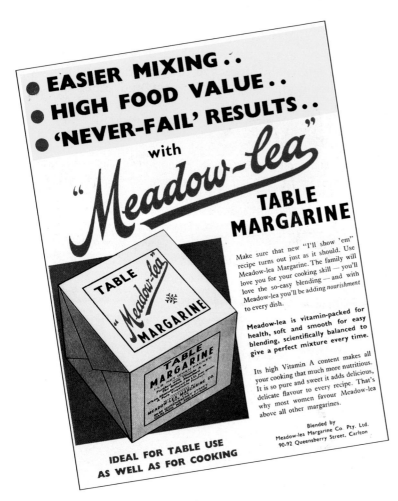

SOAP

7 lbs. fat.
6 quarts water.
2 ozs. borax.
$\frac{1}{2}$ lb. resin.
1 lb. caustic soda.

(1) Heat fat, resin, water, and borax till melted. (2) Take off fire and add caustic soda gradually, stirring all the time, then boil one hour. (3) Pour into boxes lined with wet calico and let set. (4) Cut into bars and allow to harden before using.

We also had suet, bought from the butcher. It was essential for a suet crust or a real Christmas pud. If you had a nice butcher, he'd take the meaty bits out and take the membrane off it for you, which made it less disgusting.

There was nothing disgusting about copha, which came in solid white blocks and melted down to a transparent liquid. Most baby boomers have a soft spot in their hearts (not literally I hope) for copha, because it was used to make chocolate crackles.

Of course, the baby boomer generation wasn't brought up in a fat-conscious world. We knew nothing of cholesterol or polyunsaturates. Our mothers would have thought they were being cheated if they were offered low-fat cheeses or fat-free soup. Times have changed.

Rabbit pie

This used to worry me as a child. I always expected to find an actual rabbit, intact in the pie. Do not be alarmed! This pie contains only rabbit meat and other delicious ingredients.

Ingredients

1 rabbit

water

1 bay leaf

3 large tomatoes

2 slices lean bacon

1 onion

salt and pepper

Puff pastry (use frozen pastry if you prefer)

120 g (4 oz) self-raising flour

60 g (2 oz) margarine

1 egg yolk

½ cup chilled water

squeeze of lemon juice

milk for glazing

Serves 6

Method

Put the rabbit into a saucepan and cover with water. Add the bay leaf. Boil the rabbit in water for 1 hour, or until the meat can be easily removed from the bones. Place in the pie dish and cover with thick slices of tomato. Cut the onion into rings. Chop the bacon and fry with the onion until the onion is soft. Season with salt and pepper. Place onion and bacon mixture over tomatoes.

Make the pastry by rubbing the margarine into the flour. Add the egg yolk, water and lemon to form a soft dough. Roll out to the shape of the pie dish, only bigger so there's enough to form a crust. Lay over rabbit mixture. Brush with milk and bake in a hot oven for 20 minutes.

RABBIT CASSEROLE

The rabbit played a large part in the baby boomer childhood. At the pictures we saw on newsreels the dramatic effects of rabbit plagues. The ABC *Country Hour* spent much time recounting the score of rabbits versus farmers. As a nation, we rode on the sheep's back. Australian cows had made a splendid contribution to the war effort with their butter. The poor old rabbit was nothing but a nuisance in culinary terms, an also-ran. This recipe shows just how much we underestimate this little creature.

Ingredients

1 rabbit, jointed

salted water

seasoned plain flour

1½ cups brown breadcrumbs

1 onion

herbs, salt, pepper

2 large rashers lean bacon

2 large cooking apples

1 dessertspoon brown sugar

1 cup milk

Serves 6

Method

Soak the rabbit for about 30 minutes in enough salted water to cover the rabbit. Dry, then roll the pieces in seasoned flour, and put them in the casserole dish. Chop the onion, combine it with herbs, salt and pepper, then sprinkle this over the rabbit. Sprinkle breadcrumbs over the top. Lay the bacon rashers on top. Peel the apples, cut them into quarters and arrange them on top of the bacon. Sprinkle with brown sugar and pour over the milk. Bake in a slow oven for 3 hours.

RISSOLES

This dish bears no relationship to the "rissole roll with sauce" which my husband orders from cheap eateries just to embarrass me. Real home-made rissoles may not be sophisticated, but they are nutritious and very tasty. They are also — as our mothers no doubt remember — very economical.

Ingredients

120 g (4 oz) lean mince

1 small cooked onion

1 tablespoon tomato sauce

1 teaspoon Worcester sauce

60 g (2 oz) mashed potato

1 egg

seasoned flour

Mum used to send me up the back to pick the mint for the sauce. When I was about seven I was allowed to put it through the grinder. It was the first thing I learned how to make.

Serves 6

Method

Chop the onion *very* finely and mix into the mincemeat. Add the tomato sauce, Worcester sauce and mashed potato, combining it all thoroughly. Beat the egg and work it through the mixture thoroughly. Form into 6 balls. Dip each one in seasoned flour and shallow fry until brown all over. Drain on kitchen paper and serve hot.

CORNISH PASTIES

Until I tried this recipe, I thought cornish pasties were only something you bought at the tuckshop. This is a vaguely similar but infinitely superior product.

Ingredients

300 g (9½ oz) beef steak (blade or round)

1 onion

1 tablespoon plain flour

water

2 potatoes

1 tablespoon parsley to garnish

The pastry (use frozen pastry if you prefer)

120 g (4 oz) self-raising flour

60 g (2 oz) margarine

2 tablespoons iced water

milk for glazing

Serves 6

Method

Cut the meat and the onion finely. Brown the meat and onions in a non-stick pan. Add the flour, then enough water to make gravy. Chop the potatoes into small cubes and add them to the meat and onion. Simmer gently for 20 minutes.

Make the pastry by rubbing the margarine through the flour and adding water to form a dough. Roll out on a floured board and cut into 6 circular pieces. Wet the edges lightly with milk. Spoon some of the meat mixture onto half the pastry then fold over and pinch into a frill around the edges.

Place on a baking tray and glaze with milk. Bake at 220°C (425°F) for 10 minutes, then turn down heat to 180°C (350°F) and bake a further 20 minutes. Serve hot, garnished with parsley.

The easy, thrifty way to give them

good prime meat they need

Sliced from bulk to your requirements — or in handy 8-oz. "knobs"

Juicy pork, tender beef, quality ham and veal — expertly blended and seasoned as only Andersons know how! Andersons "Cold Cut" sausages are rich in complete protein — your MOST essential food. No trouble, no cooking, **no waste!**

ANDERSONS GARLIC SAUSAGE

ANDERSONS LUNCHEON SAUSAGE

ANDERSONS FRITZ SAUSAGE

Don't accept substitutes . . . look for the name . . . Andersons!

ANDERSONS the famous name for quality, freshness, flavour...

Your family is right in wanting meat — they need it every day, the whole year round. And you are right in wanting Andersons "Cold Cut" sausages for quick, mouth-watering meals because—

● Andersons use only prime beef, pork and veal — specially selected and country-killed in their own abattoirs . . .

● Andersons maintain a non-stop delivery of fresh supplies in sparklingly-clean refrigerated vans. Their dependable freshness safeguards your family's health.

● Andersons — leaders in the meat trade for nearly fifty years — bring specialised skill, experience and quality-control to every one of their 65 famous meat products — the largest, most complete range available. Look before you buy — all genuine Andersons products carry the name Andersons.

NEW! NOW AVAILABLE

Andersons "Cold Cut" Sausages ready sliced in handy 8 oz. packets—fresh, hygienic, delicious for salads and sandwiches.

Ask for

ANDERSONS

...taste the quality difference

A58

One, two, three, four, five,
Once I caught a fish alive,
Six, seven, eight, nine, ten,
Then I let him go again.
Why did you let him go?
Because he bit my finger so.
Which finger did he bite?
This little finger on the right.

Catching fish was a baby boomer occupation for children who lived near rivers or the sea. Sometimes the cat was the only beneficiary of this activity, but there was also an occasional mother who actually knew how to cook fish.

FISH CASSEROLE

Simple and easy and the fish tastes great!

Ingredients

6 bream or flounder fillets

6 small potatoes sliced crossways in thin slices

2 large sliced tomatoes

2 cloves garlic, crushed

2 dessertspoons margarine or butter

9 green olives

Method

Put three fillets on the bottom of a casserole dish. Cover with half the sliced potatoes and tomatoes and half of the crushed garlic. Dot with butter and repeat the layers. Top off with olive slices. Cover and bake at 170°C (335°F) for 1 hour.

DEVILLED WHITEBAIT

I remember my home science teacher telling us that devilled meant *à la diable* or (for those who failed French) *to the devil*. We thought she was very daring. In fact, in this recipe it means you use a small amount of cayenne pepper. Be a devil, try it.

Ingredients

whitebait

plain flour

vegetable oil for frying

salt

cayenne pepper

Method

Blot the whitebait dry with some paper towels, then drop it onto a plate of flour. Make sure the fish are well floured, but shake each one to make sure it is not caked.

Heat the oil to a high temperature (test it by dropping a piece of bread into it; if the bread browns immediately, the oil is hot enough). Put in the fish, in a fish basket, and cook 2–3 minutes. Remove and toss on kitchen paper to drain. Sprinkle with salt and cayenne pepper. Serve with thin slices of brown bread and wedges of lemon.

Scotch haddock

I grizzled about this dish for about 15 years because I couldn't stand hardboiled eggs. That was silly. If you don't like hardboiled eggs, don't put them in. It still tastes delicious.

Ingredients

250 g (8 oz) haddock

1 tablespoon butter

½ onion, very finely chopped

1 tablespoon plain flour

250 mL (7 fl oz) milk

2 hardboiled eggs (optional)

breadcrumbs

parsley and lemon for garnish

Serves 6

Method

Steam fish for 10–15 minutes. It should be firm but flake easily. You may need to remove some skin so that the fish can be easily broken up into bite-size pieces.

Heat the butter very gently with the onion. The onion should cook, but not brown. Stir in the flour, then the milk. Keep stirring as the sauce comes to the boil and thickens. Put in the fish pieces.

Put about three-quarters of the mixture into a small casserole or other oven-proof dish. Slice the hardboiled eggs and arrange them on the top. Spoon over the rest of the mixture. Sprinkle with breadcrumbs and cook at 200°C (400°F) for 15 minutes. Serve garnished with a sprig of parsley and a wedge of lemon.

My uncle used to congratulate Mum on the lumps in the gravy. Best bit of a roast, he'd say.

I was allowed to mix the mustard. I made it too dry and had to put in more water. Then I made it too wet and had to put in more powder. It went on and on till I'd made enough for about a year's supply.

The table was always set with a white linen cloth and the good serviettes and serviette rings. Then there was salt and pepper, the gravy boat, white-sauce jug, mint sauce, mustard and a couple of bottles of Victoria Bitter.

We were Catholics. Friday meant fish. Simple as that.

I was much more enthusiastic about catching the fish than I ever was about eating it.

Mum used to cook the fish in batter that had the texture of old shoes.

The rabbitto was a great institution. He'd come round calling out "rabbitto, rabbitto". That was the best part.

The rabbitto came on Tuesdays. Other days he walked his greyhounds, which gave rise to certain suspicions.

We used to hang around waiting for mum to cut off the lamb shank. We'd fight like dogs to get it.

Mum used to send me up the back to pick the mint for the sauce. When I was about seven I was allowed to put it through the grinder. It was the first thing I learned how to make.

New! Modern! Automatic! Buy it Now!

The baby boomer childhood was the age for being modern. We children studied science with a religious fervour and deeply believed in change and improvement. We discarded the old pump flysprays for aerosols. We stopped shelling fresh peas and bought frozen ones by the kilo. We changed from ounces and pounds to grams and kilos. We went from pounds, shillings and pence to dollars and cents.

All this change had a dramatic effect on the lives of women. Before the war there had been electric gadgets, such as washing machines, vacuum cleaners and fridges. But after the war the rate at which women acquired these things was staggering. Ice chests gave way to kero fridges, to gas fridges and then to electric fridges, until the possession of these was virtually universal — and mandatory. The same thing happened with gas and electric ranges and other household appliances. Luxury appliances like dishwashers and freezers were becoming relatively common in the sixties. "Who's doing the washing up?" became a less frequent family squabble.

I remember the envy I felt when my friend's mother got a Sunbeam Mix Master with bowls in three different sizes. My mother never got one. She was probably thoroughly sick of cooking and was waiting for us all to leave home. Nor did she acquire a pop-up toaster, probably reasoning (very sensibly) that we'd simply eat more toast. But the rest of the nation seemed gripped with the passion for electric frypans, four-burner ranges, blenders, and irons that not only steamed but also spat at you.

All these gadgets began to change our eating patterns. If you didn't have to fiddle with a kerosene fridge or worry about an icebox, you obviously had more time for creative cooking. But it was more than this. Families had acquired cars, sometimes two, and so going to the shops once a week became feasible. Women were no longer limited to what they could carry home in a string bag or what the butcher and the grocer would deliver.

The opening of supermarkets had an enormous effect on our eating. Some of the stuff you wouldn't want to eat, but there was more choice and variety. We began to eat more bought icecream. Chicken became an everyday dish. Foods we had always used suddenly became more sophisticated and often better. Instant coffee replaced the dreadful coffee essence. Real coffee became widely available. You could buy dried milk that tasted okay and wasn't full of lumps that exploded in your mouth. You could buy pastry in packets.

But it was even more than that. By the end of the 1960s, we were just a tiny bit less xenophobic. Rice a Riso was probably the first "Chinese" food many of us tasted and we certainly didn't put chilli in anything Mexican. But we had begun to realise that there was more to food than meat and three vegetables, with pud to follow. Spaghetti still came out of a can and garlic made only a timid appearance in our food, but the great waves of immigrants were beginning to make an impact.

Our baby boomer mothers may, in retrospect, seem very conservative in their food tastes and their cooking methods. But in a sense, they were pioneers. By embracing the gadgetry of the post-war world with such fervour, they gave themselves more time. And with that time they took the first tentative steps to experimenting with an Australian cuisine which had changed very little since the arrival of the First Fleet.

2 WHAT'S FOR PUD, MUM?

Apple tart, strawberry tart,
Tell me the name of your sweetheart.

Pudding was a reward for eating up your vegetables, for not complaining about the meat, for not kicking your brother under the table. Only good children got pud. Sometimes it was disappointing. The worst I remember was being served plain red jelly with Carnation milk. But at the best, it was superb — crusty pies, delicately steamed puddings, the magic of lemon delicious. Now, when pudding is a rarer treat, we don't hear those cries of "What's for pud?" These recipes will revive the memory and satisfy the senses. See also "Sunday Nights", Chapter 5, for other puddings.

APPLE PIE

Apples played a big part in many baby boomer puddings. The fact that they were cheap and plentiful made them

You asked "what's for tea?" hoping it wouldn't be too bad. You asked "what's for pud?" thinking how good it would be.

popular with mothers. The fact that there were endless puddings they turned up in, made them popular with children.

Ingredients

Pastry (use frozen pastry if you prefer)

2 cups plain flour

1 pinch salt

1 dessertspoon icing sugar

180 g (6 oz) butter

1 tablespoon chilled water

Filling

1 kg (2.2 lb) Granny Smith apples

sugar to taste

30 g (1 oz) butter

3 cloves

water

Serves 6

Method

Mix flour, salt and icing sugar and rub the butter through. Add enough chilled water to form a light dough then roll out on a floured board to a thickness of about 7 mm (¼ in). Reserve a quarter of the pastry for the top. Line a pie dish with the rest leaving enough pastry round the top edges for a crust.

Peel and slice the apples. Layer them in the pie dish with small amounts of butter and a sprinkle of sugar if they are tart. Put the cloves in the middle layer and add 2 dessertspoons of water. If you are using a deep pie dish, put an egg cup (not a plastic one) in the middle to stop the pastry from sinking. Put the top on and pinch its edges together.

Bake in the oven at 220°C (425°F) until the pastry is golden brown. Serve hot with cream.

Apple pie, every Sunday lunch after the roast. It was as much part of our lives as going to Sunday school.

APPLE CRUMBLE

Our apple crumble always came with holes in the top. Some rotten child who shall remain nameless used to nick bits of crumble off the top while it was cooling in the kitchen. Keep your kids' nasty little fingers away from it and serve with icecream.

Ingredients

4 large Granny Smith apples

water

2 tablespoons golden syrup

grated rind of 1 lemon

juice of ½ lemon

1 cup self-raising flour

1 pinch salt

½ teaspoon cinnamon

½ cup brown sugar

60 g (2 oz) margarine

2 tablespoons desiccated coconut

Serves 6

Method

Stew the apples in water until soft. Mix with golden syrup, lemon rind and lemon juice. Put in a pie dish.

Mix the flour, salt, cinnamon and sugar. Rub the margarine into the mixture until it is the texture of coarse breadcrumbs. Sprinkle over the apples and sprinkle with coconut. Bake for 30 minutes at 180°C (350°F). Serve with icecream.

TABLE OF MEASURES

By a spoon is meant a rounded spoon; that is, as much above the rim of the spoon as under it.
Half a teaspoon is a level spoon.
A quarter of a spoon is a level spoon divided lengthways.
One-eighth of a spoon is half a quarter of a spoon.
One tablespoon of flour equals 1 oz.
One scant tablespoon of sugar equals 1 oz.
One dessertspoon of butter or fat equals 1 oz.
Six tablespoons of liquor equal one gill.
Four gills equal one pint.
One heaped teacup of flour equals 4 oz.
One scant teacup of sugar equals 4 oz.
One heaped large teacup of flour equals 6 oz.
One heaped breakfast cup of flour equals 8 oz.
One scant breakfast cup of sugar equals 8 oz.
Eight to ten eggs equal 1 lb.

Dad used to buy apples by the case, depending which ones were in season. Mum would curse if there were bad ones at the bottom of the box, but she'd go through them, cut out the bad bits and stew them up for the baby or for pud. We had a pie on Sunday, but the rest of the week it was just stewed apple, sometimes with custard, for pudding.

APPLE TART

Apple tart was a step up from apple pie. Apple pie was great for a family pud, but our family geared up for visitors with the rather more fancy and complex tart.

Ingredients

Pastry

150 g (5 oz) self-raising flour

30 g (1 oz) cornflour

1 pinch salt

90 g (3 oz) butter

1 egg yolk (set aside the egg white)

60 g (2 oz) sugar

Filling

4 apples

¼ cup water

rind and juice of ½ lemon

1 tablespoon butter

½ cup desiccated coconut

2 eggs—separate yolks from whites

¾ cup sugar

Serves 6

Method

Mix flour, cornflour and salt and rub the butter through. Add beaten egg yolk and sugar and mix to a dry dough. Roll out and line a pie shell with the pastry.

   Peel, core and then stew the apples with water, lemon rind and juice. Beat to a puree, add the butter, coconut, egg yolks and half a cup of sugar. Allow to cool before putting into the pastry shell. Put in the oven at 220°C (425°F) for 15–20 minutes. Beat the three egg whites stiffly to a meringue texture and add the remaining ¼ cup of sugar. Pile this onto the apple mixture and bake until the meringue is slightly brown.

STUFFED APPLES

If you want to be a real baby boomer, you can core the apples with a dolly peg. However, if you want to avoid splinters in your dessert and a faint taste of washing soda, use a good modern apple corer.

Ingredients

6 large green apples

½ cup raisins

½ cup pitted dates

½ cup brown sugar

1 teaspoon butter

½ teaspoon cinnamon

water

Serves 6

Method

Chop the raisins and dates and mix them with the brown sugar, butter and cinnamon. Core the apples, then fill them with the mixture.

Place in a pie dish and put in water so the apples are covered to about 3 cm (1 in) up their sides. Place a dot of butter on each apple and bake in the oven at 200°C (400°F) until the apples are soft — it usually takes about 45 minutes. Serve with whipped cream.

Apple on a stick,
apple on a stick,
Every time I turn around,
it makes me sick.

APPLE BUTTERSCOTCH

This dish comes with my personal 5-star recommen-
dation. I tried it after a 20-year break and found my
sensory memory cells to be absolutely intact.

Ingredients

Pastry (use frozen pastry if you prefer)

120 g (4 oz) self-raising flour

60 g (2 oz) plain flour

1 pinch salt

90 g (3 oz) butter or margarine

2 tablespoons sugar

3 tablespoons cold water

Filling

3 medium cooking apples

½ cup brown sugar

½ cup sultanas

1 teaspoon cinnamon

½ teaspoon grated lemon rind

Butterscotch glaze

60 g (2 oz) butter

½ cup brown sugar

½ cup water

Serves 6

Method

Mix the flours and salt and rub the butter through the
mixture. Mix the sugar through and then add water to
form a firm dough. Turn onto a floured board and roll to
a rectangle 30 cm x 20 cm (12 in x 8 in), about 1 cm

We hardly ever had cream to
go with things. We knew it
was too expensive.

(⅓ in) thick. Dice the apples and mix with the brown sugar, sultanas, cinnamon and grated lemon rind. Spread the filling evenly over the pastry. Roll up from the longer side and press together the edges of the pastry to seal the roll.

Put the roll on a lightly greased baking dish with the join at the bottom. With a sharp knife make a few crosswise insertions along the roll. Bake in the oven at 200°C (400°F) for 20 minutes.

For the glaze, heat butter, brown sugar and water. Pour over the apple roll. Return to the oven and bake another 10 minutes. Serve hot with cream or custard.

Mum thought she could memorise recipes. She couldn't. Sometimes the puddings were great, sometimes they were rock hard or really sloppy.

TREACLE OR JAM ROLY

This dish is for all those who endured boarding-schools in the post-war era. Perhaps this will bring back better memories.

Ingredients

150 g (5 oz) plain flour

1 level teaspoon baking powder

60 g (2 oz) suet

2 tablespoons treacle or jam

4 tablespoons breadcrumbs

1 teaspoon grated lemon rind

The sauce

1 tablespoon arrowroot

½ cup water

2 tablespoons treacle or jam

1 teaspoon lemon juice

1 dessertspoon butter

Serves 6

Method

Set a large saucepan of water to boil. Mix the flour and baking powder. Flake the suet finely and rub into the flour and baking powder. Mix to a stiff dough, knead and roll out to a rectangle. Spread the treacle or jam over it and sprinkle breadcrumbs and lemon rind on it. Wet the edges and roll up. (The roly should have the proportions of a log cake or a Swiss roll.) Sprinkle flour over a clean tea-towel. Wrap the cloth around the roly and tie securely at each end. Put into the boiling water and boil for 45 minutes. Serve with treacle or jam sauce.

To make the sauce, blend the arrowroot and water. Heat the other ingredients in a saucepan, but do not allow them to boil. Remove from the heat and stir in the arrowroot and water mixture. Return to the heat, slowly bring to the boil and simmer gently for a few minutes. Pour it over the roly just before you serve.

SPOTTED DOG

Baby boomers were brought up on the notion that civilised people don't eat dogs. As a child, this gave me a little trouble with the following dessert. Thankfully, I am now over my childhood inhibitions and can now eat spotted dog with the best.

Ingredients

Suet crust

100 g (3½ oz) self-raising flour

100 g (3½ oz) fresh white breadcrumbs

100 g (3½ oz) shredded or grated suet

125 ml (4 fl oz) water

1 pinch salt

Filling

150 g (5 oz) of mixed sultanas, currants, raisins and peel

Serves 6

Method

Mix together the ingredients for the crust to form a soft dough. Roll out to a length of 60 cm (24 in) and about half as wide. Sprinkle the fruit over it and then roll up lengthwise to make a sausage. Wrap in a pudding cloth (a strong tea-towel is a good substitute) and secure with string. Boil for 45 minutes. Serve with custard.

My mother didn't make pudding. I couldn't wait to get to boarding-school to taste bread and butter pudding. In retrospect, I would have preferred to skip boarding-school.

BREAD AND BUTTER PUDDING

Another boarding-school dish. This one has been resurrected as a trendy dish and is now recognised as a fine and delicate pud. It is served at many upmarket restaurants, hotels and the very best dinner parties, including my own.

Ingredients

12 slices white bread

50 g (1½ oz) currants

120 g (4 oz) sugar

500 ml (16 fl oz) milk

3 egg yolks

1 whole egg

nutmeg

apricot jam for glaze

Serves 6

Method

Grease an ovenproof pudding dish, then cut the crusts from the bread and cut each slice diagonally. Arrange the slices in the pudding dish with currants sprinkled between each layer.

Dissolve the sugar in the milk. Whisk 3 egg yolks and the beaten egg and add to the milk and sugar. Pour over the bread slices. Sprinkle with nutmeg.

Cook in a double dish with about 2.5 cm (1 in) of water at 180°C (350°F) for 45 minutes. Brush with apricot jam and cook for a further 15 minutes. Allow to rest 10 minutes before serving. Serve with thick cream.

cocoa... the added touch that means so much

Photograph of Cadbury Bournville advertisement used by permission of Cadbury Confectionery Australia

CHOCOLATE PUD

Guaranteed to be feverishly consumed by adults and children alike.

Ingredients

60 g (2 oz) butter

½ cup caster sugar

1 cup self-raising flour

1 tablespoon cocoa (unsweetened)

1 egg

½ cup milk

Sauce

1 tablespoon cocoa (unsweetened)

⅓ cup caster sugar

1 cup hot water

Serves 6

Method

Melt the butter with the sugar in a saucepan. Sift the flour and cocoa over the top, then beat in the egg and milk. Grease an ovenproof dish (a soufflé dish is excellent) and pour in the pudding.

To make the sauce, mix the sugar and cocoa and sift it over the pudding. Then carefully pour the hot water over it. (To avoid making holes in the pud, pour the hot water over the back of a spoon.) Cook at 180°C (350°F) for 35 minutes. Serve with cream or icecream.

WARM QUINCE CAKE

The quince is still a much-neglected fruit. As a child, I loved the way it started off yellow and then turned deep pink. I still think the colour is fabulous, as well as the taste.

Ingredients

2 big quinces, peeled, cored and cut into slices about 1 cm
(½ in) thick

1 cup water

4 tablespoons sugar

1 tablespoon lemon juice

½ teaspoon cinnamon

Sponge

30 g (1 oz) butter

½ cup caster sugar

1 pinch salt

½ cup self-raising flour

1 large egg

Serves 4

Method

Put quinces in a saucepan with water, lemon juice, sugar
and cinnamon and simmer gently until the quinces are a
deep red—this usually takes about 40 minutes. Drain and
allow to cool.

To make the sponge, melt the butter in a saucepan and
pour into a bowl. Add sugar and salt. Gently mix in the
flour. Beat the egg and fold in gently.

Grease an ovenproof pudding dish. Arrange the quinces
in the bottom and then spoon the sponge mixture over
them. Bake at 200°C (400°F) for 20 minutes or until
golden on top. Serve with cold custard.

Steamed Pudding with Golden Syrup

Golden syrup used to be a standard ingredient in any baby boomer kitchen. It went into an enormous number of cakes, biscuits and puds. It probably had some medicinal purpose. It's worth lashing out on a tin to savour the delights of this excellent winter pudding.

Ingredients

90 g (3 oz) butter

3 tablespoons caster sugar

1 egg

1 cup self-raising flour

⅓ cup milk

1 teaspoon vanilla

3 tablespoons golden syrup

Serves 4

Method

Cream butter and sugar. Beat in the egg. Fold in the flour alternately with milk and vanilla.

Put the golden syrup in the bottom of a 4-cup pudding basin. (Test the capacity with water. If you don't have a pudding basin, an ordinary ceramic basin will do, although it may be harder to cover it.) Spoon the pudding mixture on top of the golden syrup. Cover with a lid or pudding cap, or use greaseproof paper or aluminium foil fastened with string or a large rubber band. Put the pudding bowl in a large saucepan with about 10 cm (4 in) of water. The water should come about halfway up the sides of the bowl. Simmer gently for about 1¼ hours. Remove from the water, let it rest for 5 minutes and then turn out onto a dish. Serve with cream or icecream.

"Magical!"

JOAN WINFIELD OF WHITE WINGS TEST KITCHEN SAYS:

A baked dessert that makes its own sauce!"

White Wings Sponge Pudding Mix

BUTTERSCOTCH

CHOCOLATE

NEW SUMMER FLAVOUR LEMON DELICIOUS

You never *saw* anything like them — magical mouth-melting puddings that form their own sauce as they bake.
You never *tasted* anything like them — cake as light as home-made butter-sponge, sitting pretty over lashings of rich sauce!
You never *served* anything like them — second helping sweets that add a party touch to meals, yet save you so much time, so much trouble. You can be sure they're good — they're White Wings.

1. SURPRISE! You get the Sponge Mix and the Sauce Mix both in the one packet.

2. SURPRISE! Just sprinkle your dry sauce portion over the sponge batter, no further mixing required!

3. SURPRISE! Pour boiling water over a spoon onto sponge batter – don't stir – pop in oven.

THE AUSTRALIAN WOMEN'S WEEKLY — December 2, 1959

LEMON DELICIOUS

White Wings

self-saucing

Sponge pudding MIX

It floats on sauce that starts on top and cooks right through

LEMON DELICIOUS

This is a magic pudding. I still find it fantastic that it starts off as a single substance and separates into two layers.

Ingredients

2 level tablespoons butter

¾ cup sugar

2 level tablespoons self-raising flour

1 pinch salt

grated rind of 1 large or 2 medium lemons

2 eggs, separated

1 cup milk

Method

Cream the butter and sugar. Add the flour and the salt. Add grated lemon rind, egg yolk and milk. Fold in the stiffly beaten egg white. Bake in a double dish (stand it in water) for 40 minutes at 175°C (340°F).

BANANAS IN RUM SAUCE

Overripe bananas went into banana cakes, banana pancakes and this recipe. This dish is well worth making even if you have to buy overripe bananas especially.

Ingredients

4 bananas

1 dessertspoon butter

1 cup rum

½ cup brown sugar

½ cup cream

Serves 4

Method

Slice bananas lengthways and then in half. Fry them lightly in butter. Add rum and sugar and cook gently until bananas are cooked but not mushy. Remove from heat and stir in the cream. Serve immediately.

STIRRED CUSTARD

I always wished my mother had been modern enough in outlook to buy custard powder. Instead, she insisted on the trauma and drama of custard made in a double sauce-pan. Having now tried the custard powder variety, I understand her old-fashioned ways. Quite simply, it tastes real.

Ingredients

375 mL (13 fl oz) milk

1 egg

1 tablespoon sugar

½ teaspoon vanilla

1 pinch nutmeg

Method

Warm the milk in a double saucepan. Don't use an aluminium saucepan as it may give your custard a greyish tinge. Beat egg and sugar until thick and creamy and add to the milk. Stir continuously until the custard thickens. This may take 10–20 minutes, but it is best to do it slowly. Do not allow the custard to boil or it will curdle. Add the essence and serve with a sprinkle of nutmeg or use as an accompaniment to other dishes.

3 SUMMER PUDDINGS

I loved summer puddings, mainly because Mum would sometimes buy real icecream from the shop to go with them.

Icecream and jelly,
a punch in the belly.
Fruit and nuts,
a punch in the guts.

Given the amount of time our mothers spent in the kitchen, it's amazing they had the enthusiasm to create a different dessert every night, especially during the long Australian summer. Some of them, like home-made ice-cream, are not recommended, but flummeries, creams, and the more grandiose — like trifle — bring back wonderful memories.

PASSIONFRUIT FLUMMERY

I've always loved the name and have many fond memories of it as a dessert. I promise that flummery is everything you remember.

Ingredients

2 level dessertspoons gelatine

1 cup water

juice of 2 oranges and 1 lemon

1½ cups sugar

1 tablespoon flour

8 passionfruit

Serves 6

Method

Combine the gelatine, water, fruit juice and sugar. Heat slowly in a saucepan until the gelatine is dissolved. Add the flour, blended with water, stir in and bring to the boil. Simmer gently for 2 minutes. Put into a large basin and let stand until it begins to set. Add the passionfruit pulp and beat for 10 minutes. Pour into a mould. When set, turn out, and serve with whipped cream or icecream.

It really depended on Mum. There weren't any frozen puddings or instant puddings in the supermarkets. In fact, there weren't any supermarkets.

SPANISH CREAM

My mother's recipe for this is preceded by the warning that "Spanish cream is improved by covering it with apricot jam and topping with whipped cream". This caution shook my faith in my childhood memories. Maybe this wasn't the sophisticated dessert I had imagined. However, I tried it and found to my delight that the apricot jam is not necessary. You might not want to serve Spanish cream every night of your life, but it's a simple and easy summer dessert that will bring joy to the hearts of baby boomers.

Ingredients

2 eggs

½ cup sugar

600 mL (1 pint) milk

15 g (½ oz) gelatine

vanilla essence

Serves 6

Method

Whisk the eggs and sugar together until the sugar is dissolved. Heat a little of the milk and dissolve the gelatine in it. Combine this with the rest of the milk, then the egg mixture. Stir thoroughly, then heat gently in a saucepan but do not boil the mixture or it will curdle. (If it does curdle, all is not lost — see recipe for Angels' food.) The mixture will thicken gradually. Add the vanilla. Pour into a mould to set. Serve cold with whipped cream.

ANGELS' FOOD (OR WHAT TO DO IF YOUR SPANISH CREAM CURDLES)

Method

Follow the recipe for Spanish cream, but boil the milk and egg mixture so it *does* curdle. Take it off the heat. Take another 2 eggs and separate them. Beat up the whites to a stiff froth. Allow the milk mixture to cool a little, add the yolks with a teaspoon of lemon juice, then fold in the eggwhites. Allow to set in the fridge.

LEMON MERINGUE PIE

This was definitely a party dish in our household. I had a friend whose mother made it every week. That was the sort of family to be born into!

Ingredients

Pastry

120 g (4 oz) butter

180 g (6 oz) self-raising flour

chilled water

Filling

60 g (2 oz) butter

240 g (8 oz) sugar

¾ cup water

1 dessertspoon cornflour

2 eggs, separated

juice of 2 lemons

Serves 6

Method

Rub the butter into the flour, then add chilled water to make a light dough. Roll out to line a tart plate about 25 cm (10 in) in diameter. Bake in the oven at 220°C (425°F) for 15–20 minutes until browned. Leave to cool.

Put the butter, half the sugar and half the water into a saucepan to boil. Blend the cornflour with the remaining water and add it to the mixture. Bring to the boil again and stir until it thickens. Allow to cool, then add the beaten egg yolks and lemon juice. When it is cold, spoon mixture into the pastry case. Whip the egg whites to a stiff froth, add the remaining sugar gradually and continue whipping until they form stiff peaks. Cover the lemon mixture with the meringue, creating peaks over the surface. Place in the oven at a low temperature and bake for 1 hour until the meringue is crisp and pale brown.

We never had just fresh fruit for dessert. It would have seemed a bit slack. It had to be whipped up into something.

MARSHMALLOW MACAROONS

The use of sherry in desserts was somewhat daring and indicated an *adults only* dessert.

Ingredients

1 packet marshmallows

½ cup sherry

300 mL (½ pint) cream

McWILLIAM'S *Cream* SHERRY

McWilliam's Cream Sherry wins more friends every day. It is a specially selected sweet sherry with a smooth, creamy body, so mild and mellow that it's right for every occasion. McWilliam's Cream Sherry is truly versatile, so for your own enjoyment, and when friends drop in, keep McWilliam's Cream Sherry in your home.

SHERRY ON THE ROCKS

Simply place two ice cubes in a glass and pour over 2 or 3 ozs. of McWilliam's Cream Sherry.

OM THE PROUDEST GRAPES IN AUSTRALIA

AUSTRALIAN WOMEN'S WEEKLY – April 6, 1960   Page 1

In winter, we had pudding in ceramic bowls with a little crisscross design round the edge. In summer, Mum used glass dishes.

1 packet macaroons (if you're keen, make them — see Bikkies and scones, Chapter 7, page 131).

1 punnet strawberries

Cream came out of a tin. There was a lump in the middle and runny stuff round the lump.

Serves 6

Method

Soak marshmallows overnight in sherry. Just before serving, whip the cream to a stiff consistency. Crush the macaroons and combine with cream. Add the marshmallows and the hulled strawberries. Serve in trifle glasses.

RICE CUSTARD

Still a great way of using the leftover rice from the curry. A wonderful, simple, creamy dessert.

Ingredients

1 cup cooked rice (soft and moist, not dry)

400 mL (14 fl oz) milk

½ cup sugar

1 egg

1 egg yolk

3 drops vanilla

nutmeg

Serves 4

Method

Beat the milk and sugar and add the eggs, beating well. Then add the rice and vanilla. Grease a pie dish. Pour the mixture in and sprinkle nutmeg over the top. Stand the pie dish in a baking dish of cold water to prevent the custard from curdling while it cooks. Bake in the oven at 180°C (350°F) for about 30 minutes or until set.

TRIFLE

In the country town where my grandparents lived, the cake shop frequently displayed a large sign: "Stale sponge available". I always assumed this was a cut-price special until my grandmother told me that *stale* sponge was the only sort of sponge to use in a trifle.

Ingredients

1 stale spongecake

raspberry jam

8 small macaroons

300 mL (½ pint) sherry

1 small bowl firm red jelly

500 mL (16 fl oz) custard

---

300 mL (½ pint) cream

Serves 6

Method

Cut the sponge into fingers and spread with the jam. Line a deep glass bowl with fingers of sponge, coming a little way up the side. Arrange the macaroons around the bowl. Pour the sherry over it. Cut the jelly into small cubes and arrange over the cake. Cover with custard. Just before serving, whip the cream and pile on top of the trifle. Decorate with chopped walnuts if desired. (This can also be made in individual trifle dishes.)

We never had people to dinner, except the rels. They didn't make any difference to the type of meal we had, except when my aunty came. Mum felt the need to impress her, so she'd whip up a trifle or a pavlova.

I like Aeroplane JELLY

My boyfriend gave me peaches,
My boyfriend gave me pears,
My boyfriend gave me sixpence,
And kissed me up the stairs.

SAGO CREAM

Large sets of canisters used to come with one canister marked *sago*. It's now an uncommon item to find in a kitchen. However, it is available in supermarkets. Sago cream lives!

Ingredients

2 eggs, separated

2 cups milk

2 tablespoons sugar

2 heaped tablespoons sago

Serves 4–6

Method

Beat the egg whites until stiff. Combine the yolks with the milk, then add the sugar and the sago. Heat slowly, stirring constantly, until the mixture thickens. Do not allow it to boil. Fold the beaten egg whites through it. Pour into a glass dish or mould and leave to set. Serve cold with fruit and cream.

BLANCMANGE

There are others of my generation who remember blancmange with more affection than I do. I hunted down this recipe, which looked rather more luxurious than the others dubbed *For Invalids,* and found that it is a simple and pleasant dessert. The vanilla bean adds a touch of class. One thing that has always puzzled me — do the French really eat blancmange too?

Ingredients

500 mL (16 fl oz) milk

1 vanilla bean

2 tablespoons cornflour

1 tablespoon water

3 tablespoons sugar

120 mL (4 fl oz) cream

Serves 4

Method

Heat the milk with the vanilla bean. Blend the cornflour with water and stir it into the milk. Add the sugar. Continue stirring until the mixture boils and while it simmers for another 5 minutes. Stir in the cream and pour into a serving bowl. Put into the fridge to set and serve with whipped cream.

Dancing dolly's got no
  sense,
Bought four eggs for
  eighteen pence.
The eggs went bad,
  dolly went mad.
Dancing dolly's got no
  sense.

SALAD DAYS OF THE FIFTIES

There were good things and there were bad things about salads in the 1950s. Let's look at the good things first.

First, tomatoes were tomatoes. We knew that, because we grew them up the back in the vegie plot and nurtured them with the compost made from kitchen scraps and manure.

We knew lettuces were ours too. We defended them in a nightly and eternal battle against slugs and snails. Cabbages, carrots, potatoes and numerous other vegetables were also home-grown. If they weren't, you knew they still came out of the earth, not from a laboratory.

Some of the things like beetroot, we couldn't accept as raw vegetables. We cooked them up in the pressure-cooker, with a bit of sugar and a dash of vinegar, until they tasted just like the tinned variety. "Remarkable," our mothers said proudly, "can't tell the difference."

Lots of the salad came out of tins. Limp asparagus, or asparagus cuts. Beetroot, carrots and peas. And salad dressing — it was a mixture of condensed milk, vinegar and mustard. People called it mayonnaise. Our lettuces were usually home grown, but some cooks shredded them so finely that they may as well have been tinned.

The food we served with our salads wasn't too great either. Processed cheese in silver paper was the only cheese we really knew about. If you were squeamish, you picked the round, white bits of fat out of your Devon. Sometimes, it was camp pie, which was just too horrible to contemplate. Were war-time army rations being used up? The bread was always white. Later, it came sliced, in waxed paper wrappers. You couldn't buy fresh bread on weekends so it was always stale when you went on picnics.

Printed with the permission of Kraft Foods Limited

A good salad was an arrangement, a work of culinary artistry. Delicately sliced tomatoes nestled in lettuce leaves. Cheese sliced and arranged in a fan shape. Tinned asparagus spears, nattily displayed. When guests came, you put bright red and green pickled onions on toothpicks and stuck them on a grapefruit. This was a proud centrepiece. If you were sophisticated, you offered a bowl of soapy olives.

Salt was important, too. The natural taste of the fresh homegrown vegies must have been wonderful, but we made sure we didn't notice it because we covered everything with salt.

Ah, the salad days of the fifties. But at least the tomatoes were real.

4 LOVELY HOT SOUP

Keep the kettle boiling,
Do not miss a loop,
Keep the kettle boiling,
Else you'll get no soup.

Few families had soup as part of the main meal, except on special occasions when there were guests. More frequently, it was a meal in itself, for lunch on weekends or school holidays.

PEA AND HAM SOUP

Our mothers made pea and ham soup partly out of a sense of economy. It's still dirt cheap, but so long as you make sure your bacon bones aren't fatty, it can also rate as a health food.

This soup is best made in a pressure-cooker, which speeds up cooking time tremendously. A pressure-cooker is a wonderful investment for any soup-maker. However, few baby boomers have bought these invaluable kitchen aids, having been scared out of their wits in their childhood by exploding cookers. It was rather like waiting for the whales to spout. The modern variety is less dramatic and does not behave in this unpredictable fashion.

Ingredients

4 meaty bacon bones

---

250 g (8 oz) split peas

1.5 L (2½ pt) stock (If you want a short-cut, boil up a couple of stock cubes with 2 onions, some herbs, a few sticks of celery and some black peppercorns; strain off the solids and you'll have a wonderful stock.)

There was a Sunday night play on the ABC. We'd have our tea late and listen to it with our soup plates on our knees.

Serves 6–8

Method

If you don't have a pressure-cooker, you will need to soak the split peas overnight. Then put them in the saucepan with the bacon bones and stock and simmer for 2–3 hours on a very gentle heat, stirring occasionally. If you are making it in a pressure-cooker, bring to the boil and cook on high pressure for 25 minutes. Next, remove the bacon bones and meat. Take the meat off the bones and cut finely, removing as much fat as possible. Allow the soup to cool so remaining fat can be skimmed off the top. Return the meat to the soup, heat and serve with toast or croutons (see page 78).

We had soup out of a tin. It seemed far more sophisticated than the home-made stuff.

Dad would get home from Mass and say "Thank God that's over for the week. Let's have soup for tea". We did, every Sunday night. What sort of soup depended on the vegetables in season.

TOMATO SOUP

As a child, my tomato soup came courtesy of Mr Heinz. I still have a great fondness for the tinned variety.

My aunt used to make what she termed "real tomato soup" and for this she used preserved tomatoes which she had bottled in summer. I confess that I don't know her recipe, but I do know that she pureed it and sieved it to make it as much like the tinned variety as possible. The following recipe is more an attempt to recapture the spirit of hot tomato soup on a cold night than an authentic version of soup as served in the fifties.

Ingredients

2 large onions

1 tablespoon olive oil

500 mL (16 fl oz) tomato puree

1 cup dry white wine

1 cup good strong stock

Serves 6

Method

Chop the onion very finely. Using a large saucepan, fry the onion in the olive oil until soft. Add the other ingredients and stir as they come to the boil. Depending on the thickness of the tomatoes, you may have to simmer it until it is thicker, or thin it by adding water.

MUSHROOM SOUP

In the fifties, a day in the country always meant looking for mushrooms. Finding them meant mushrooms on toast or mushroom soup for tea. Modern fertilisers have made field mushrooms a rarity in the Australian countryside.

Ingredients

300 g (9½ oz) mushrooms (big black ones give a better taste in soup)

New Maggi Tomato Soup: plump tomatoes fresh-from-the-vine . . . tenderly flavoured with the sweetness of the sun . . . gently seasoned . . . that's the flavour secret of new MAGGI

1½ tablespoons butter
2 tablespoons plain flour
500 mL (16 fl oz) milk
2 tablespoons sour cream

Serves 6

Method

Chop the mushrooms into chunky pieces. If the skin is tough and leathery remove it and discard stalks. If the mushrooms are young and tender, the skins and stalks can be used, although the stalks should be chopped finely. Fry the mushrooms lightly in the butter, then set them aside in a dish. Keep the butter on a low heat and stir in the flour. Gradually add the milk till the mixture thickens, stirring to avoid lumps. Add the mushrooms and simmer very gently for about 5 minutes. Just before serving, stir in the sour cream. Serve with hot bread or croutons (see page 78).

Mabel, Mabel,
Set the table,
Don't forget, the salt and
     pepper.

MULLIGATAWNY SOUP

I've always been in love with the name. It's a great soup, too.

Ingredients

1 dessertspoon oil

400 g (12 oz) of scrag-end mutton or lamb chopped into small pieces with fat removed

1 large onion sliced into rings

1 sliced carrot

1 large cooking apple, peeled and diced

1 tablespoon of your favourite curry powder or paste

juice of ½ lemon

1 L (1¾ pints) chicken stock

Serves 6

Method

Heat the oil in a large saucepan with a heavy base. Brown the meat and the onion. Add the carrot and apple, curry and lemon and stir until they are combined. Add the stock and simmer for 1½ hours. Remove the meat. Put the liquid through the blender. Remove any gristle or bone from the meat. Reheat with the stock.

VEGETABLE BROTH

Another economical and healthy recipe! Delicious and easy to make.

Ingredients

2 big, meaty soup bones

2 L (3½ pints) water

60 g (2 oz) barley

2 big carrots

2 big onions

1 turnip

3 sticks celery

2 dessertspoons chopped parsley

salt and pepper

Serves 6–8

Method

Put the bones into a saucepan with the water and bring to the boil. If you do this in a pressure-cooker, it will take only 30 minutes. Otherwise, you will need to boil it for 2–3 hours.

Remove the bones from the stock. Cut the meat from the bones and remove any fat or gristle. Chop finely and set aside. If you allow the stock to cool, the fat will form a white crust on the surface which can be removed easily. However, if you don't have time, skim off the fat with a spoon.

Put the meat back into the stock. Add the barley and the vegetables, chopped into small chunks. Cook slowly for 1 hour. Season as needed. Sprinkle each serving with chopped parsley.

One potato, two potato, three potato four,
Five potato, six potato, seven potato more.

OXTAIL SOUP

As a child, oxtail soup used to conjure up visions of poor tail-less oxen wandering sadly about the countryside. Now I know better and am able to enjoy oxtail soup without this horrid picture in my mind.

Ingredients

1 oxtail

2 onions

30 g (1 oz) safflower oil

1 tablespoon plain flour

1 carrot

2 sticks celery

500 mL (16 fl oz) water

1 teaspoon mixed herbs

salt

coarse ground black pepper

parsley for garnish

Method

Slice up the onions and fry them in the oil. Joint the oxtail (cut through at each joint with a sharp knife), coat

SECTION 1

BEEF AND BONE STOCK

Suitable for Vegetable Soup.
• ½ lb. Leg of Beef • 3d. worth of Bones
• Salt and Pepper • 1 small Onion • 1
Carrot • Stick of Celery • Sprig of
Parsley • 6 Peppercorns • 3 pts. cold
Water.

METHOD: Chop meat and bones small, add all other ingredients, finely chopped, to water. Simmer 2 hours. Remove any
scum that rises. Strain before using.
COPYRIGHT

with flour, and fry it with the onions. Cut up the other vegetables and add them to the pan with the water, herbs, salt and pepper. Simmer for 3 hours or pressure-cook for 45 minutes. Strain and allow the stock to cool. Skim off the fat. Thicken the stock by adding the flour mixed to a paste with cold water. Take the meat off the bones, dice finely and add to the stock. Serve very hot with a sprinkling of finely chopped parsley.

Mother's in the kitchen,
Doing a bit of stitching,
Father's in the butcher's
Cutting up the meat.
And baby's in the cradle . . .
Fast asleep.

BROWN ONION SOUP

French onion it isn't. Please remember we're baby boomers. A good, tasty, simple soup.

Ingredients

1 kg (2.2 lb) brown onions

60 g (2 oz) butter

2 tablespoons plain flour

1 L (1¾ pints) beef stock

2 large potatoes

chives for garnish

Serves 6

Method

Chop the onions into rings and fry them in the butter. Sprinkle with flour and blend it into the butter. Add the stock slowly, stirring until it comes to the boil. Simmer gently. Peel and dice the potatoes and add to the stock. Cook slowly until tender. Garnish with chives.

Croutons to serve with soup

If you want to recapture real 1950s style and spirit, cut your croutons with cookie cutters so that you can serve your soup with stars, Christmas trees and deckled edges.

Croutons are best made with stale, sliced white bread. Cut the crusts off the bread and then cut each slice diagonally.

If you don't mind a high calorie load, the croutons can then be fried in a mixture of butter and oil until crisp and brown. Drain on kitchen paper and serve hot.

Low-calorie croutons can be made without fat. Cut the bread and then dip the pieces in stock. Then place the bread on a well-greased oven tray and put into a hot oven until crisp and brown.

Modern **KITCHEN BEAUTY**

- REMOVABLE OVEN INTERIOR

- COMBINED GRILL AND WARMING CUPBOARD

- NON-TILTING OVEN SHELVES

- PLUG-IN TYPE HOTPLATES

- FOUR-HEAT BOILING PLATE

Every feature of a G.E.C. Electric Range is aimed at increasing the pleasure of cooking and making it a truly trouble-free operation. You'll get **cleaner, cooler** and more **economical** cooking with a G.E.C. Electric Range. Write for Catalogue showing models available.

Cook with a **G.E.C. ELECTRIC RANGE**

Call for a demonstration at our Showrooms

BRITISH GENERAL ELECTRIC CO. PTY. LTD.
104-114 CLARENCE STREET, SYDNEY.

FAMILY MEALS

HOW TO SET A TABLE

Spotless napery and highly-polished glass and china add greatly to the enjoyment of a well-cooked meal. Whether tablecloths or table mats are used is a matter of personal preference.

What is known as a "cover" is placed for each person. This consists of the necessary supply of cutlery, silver, glass and a table-napkin.

These are placed thus: on the right-hand side (from right to left), soup spoon, fish knife, large knife, dessertspoon. On the left-hand side (reading from left), fish fork, large fork, dessert fork. Although a fork only is used for most desserts, a spoon is usually included in the "cover."

Glasses are arranged on the right-hand side—usually a tumbler and 2 wineglasses to each "cover."

Extra cutlery, glasses, plates, together with finger-bowls and dessert dishes, should be placed on the side-board or side-table.

We all had a silver serviette ring with our name engraved on it. You had to keep your serviette for the whole week. If you were a messy child like me, it was pretty disgusting by the end of the week.

My job was to set the table. We had placemats, cutlery for every course, serviettes, salt and pepper, mats for the hot things, the gravy boat, sugar, bread and butter. It was daunting for a seven-year-old.

We always said grace at the beginning of dinner. Not breakfast or lunch. Maybe they were less God-given.

We started off with a little table and a little family. But the babies kept coming. We added on the card table at one end and the highchair for the latest baby. It was awful sitting at the card table because you were lower than everyone else.

We didn't have enough chairs. We had to use wooden fruit boxes.

Mealtimes were really strict. You got rapped over the knuckles if you misbehaved.

Mum kept a wooden spoon by the table. You got whacked if you refused to eat your food or did the wrong thing.

Mealtimes were great. Dad used to joke a lot, I think because he'd been to the pub on the way home. Mum was just pleased he was home.

The dog wasn't allowed in at mealtimes, but he'd somehow secrete himself under the table. A great way to dispose of unwanted food.

We had to eat up everything on our plates. Or stay there until we did. And no pudding unless you were quick about it.

We were reminded about the starving children in India. For a long time, I thought it was a threat to send me there unless I ate my vegetables. Even now, I don't see the connection.

We had six very noisy kids and two very garrulous parents. We all talked all the time, all through the meal at the top of our voices. It was great.

Printed with the permission of Kraft Foods Limited

HOW TO FOLD TABLE-NAPKINS

Elaborately-folded table-napkins are not much in favor nowadays, but sometimes are called for. Here are directions for two simple designs:

The Pocket Design is handy for holding pieces of bread, pulled bread, or rolls. Take a square table-napkin, and fold top and bottom corners to centre. Turn table-napkin over, and fold other two corners to centre. Now fold each of the four corners to the centre. Turn table-napkin over, and again fold the four corners to the centre. Turn table-napkin over once more, and again turn all four corners to the centre. Press well, turn table-napkin over again, and raise the corners.

Lily Leaf—Fold table-napkin over from right to left, then up from lower edge to top. Place it before you, and fold either side over. Then turn the ends under. Now take each of the points, and pull up as a leaf.

There was a lot of clattering of plates and laughing about the food. Mum's soufflés were a big joke because they always went flat. On the other hand, her doughnuts, which were just fried cake, were revered.

Mealtimes were training time. We had to wait till grace was said and Dad started to eat. We learnt to pass the salt to the adults and make sure they got the vegies and gravy first. If we wanted to leave the table, we had to ask to be excused. At the end of the meal, we had to thank Mum whether we liked the food or not.

"Who farted?" It seemed to happen so often and was so embarrassing. I think it was all the laxatives we were dosed with.

5 SUNDAY NIGHTS

Pease pudding hot, pease pudding cold,
Pease pudding in the pot, nine days old.
Some like it hot, some like it cold,
Some like it in the pot, nine days old.

Sunday night was the night for leftovers, for snacks, for having your tea in front of the fire, listening to the radio. Sunday nights were magic.

WELSH RAREBIT

When my mother was tired and frazzled we used to have grilled cheese on toast. Welsh rarebit takes more time, but is well worth it.

This is best served on thick slices of brown or white toast. The toast does not have to be buttered.

Ingredients

300 g (9½ oz) tasty cheddar cheese, grated

2 tablespoons milk

1 pinch mustard

1 tablespoon dry sherry

1 tablespoon Worcester sauce

1 pinch cayenne pepper

parsley for garnish

Serves 4

Method

In a thick saucepan, combine all the ingredients over a low heat. Stir gently. Do not allow to boil. Pour over freshly made toast. Garnish with parsley.

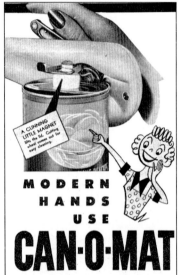

MACARONI CHEESE

My brother used to put tomato sauce on his macaroni cheese. Personally, I recommend it served plain.

Ingredients

250 g (8 oz) macaroni noodles

2 tablespoons butter

2 tablespoons plain flour

1 L (1¾ pints) milk

250 g (8 oz) tasty cheese, grated

Serves 6

Method

Cook the macaroni in boiling water until tender, but still firm. Melt the butter, blend in the flour, then add the milk. Bring to the boil to make a white sauce. Add the thoroughly drained macaroni and about half the cheese. Put in a pie dish and sprinkle the rest of the cheese over the top. Bake for about 15 minutes until the cheese is brown.

POTATO FRITTERS

This is an excellent way to use up cold boiled potatoes or roast potatoes. If you are using roast potatoes, you will have to remove the outside and use just the white flesh of the potato. If you don't have any leftovers, simply boil, bake or microwave enough potatoes and remove the skins. However, before you add the other ingredients, the potatoes should be cold.

Ingredients

700 g (1 lb 8 oz) cold, skinned potatoes

salt and pepper

2 eggs

1 tablespoon plain flour

vegetable oil

parsley for garnish

Printed with the permission of Kraft Foods Limited

Serves 6 to 8

Method

Mash the potatoes and season with salt and pepper. Beat the eggs and add them to the potatoes. Then add the flour, making sure the ingredients are thoroughly mixed. The mixture should be the consistency of pastry, so that it can be rolled out. If it is too wet, add a little more flour. Roll it out to an even thickness of 1.5 cm (½ in). Cut out with a biscuit-cutter and fry in the oil on each side until brown. Garnish with parsley — they are also delicious served with grilled bacon.

Bubble and squeak

Bubble and squeak is supposed to use up leftover cabbage and potato. However, starting bubble and squeak from scratch is worth the trouble.

Ingredients

1 cup cold cooked cabbage

2 or more cold cooked potatoes

leftover cooked onions, pumpkin, or parsnip

1 egg

salt and pepper

a little oil

Serves 4–6

Method

Chop the cabbage into short pieces. Mash the potatoes well. Chop onions finely and mash other vegetables. Put the vegetables and the egg into a bowl with salt and pepper, and combine the ingredients lightly, taking care not to turn the vegetables into a mush. Form into large patties. Heat the oil in a frypan and fry the patties on both sides, making sure that they brown but do not burn. Serve hot garnished with parsley — they are also delicious with a slice of bacon.

CAULIFLOWER CHEESE

Cauliflower cheese was usually a thrifty way to use up the leftover cauliflower from Sunday's dinner. Some years, when too many cauliflowers grew in the vegetable garden, it was regular Sunday night fare.

Ingredients

½ cauliflower

1 tablespoon butter

1 heaped tablespoon plain flour

300 mL (9 oz) milk

100 g (3½ oz) grated cheddar cheese

Serves 4

Method

Steam the cauliflower for about 10 minutes. It should be just a little firmer than usual for serving on its own. Cut it into large chunks and place in an ovenproof dish.

Melt the butter in a saucepan. Blend in the flour. Add the milk and stir until it boils and thickens. Add about half the grated cheese to the sauce and pour over the cauliflower. Sprinkle the rest of the cheese on top. Bake in

SECTION **D**

Opening Screw-top Bottles!

Obstinate these, at times. They'll yield to one or other of these operations. If the cap is small enough, pinch it in the nut-crackers and turn; tops of larger bottles will respond to sand-paper in a firm grip, or else hold a lighted match under the rim for a few seconds (mind your fingers!). For contents that will not spoil by heating, stand the bottle or jar in a dish of very hot water for a few minutes.

WHITE WINGS Self Raising FLOUR.
One bake will PROVE it's better!

SECTION G

Vegetable Wrinkles!

Pop a piece of bread in the saucepan with your cauliflower. It helps to take up the odour, also to remove any discolouration. Baked parsnips will cook quicker and taste much nicer if you pour boiling water over them before popping them in beside the roast.

Bake with WHITE WINGS, so people will say "Ah—what a wonderful cook!"

a moderate oven for 20 minutes and then turn up to high for 5 minutes so the cheese browns.

BAKED POTATOES

These are appearing at fast food counters, served with all sorts of fancy bits and pieces. I believe this good old faithful tastes better than any of the new toppings.

Ingredients

1 large potato per person

milk

butter

salt

grated cheese

Method

Scrub the potatoes well. Put on a baking tray and bake in a moderate oven until cooked — usually 1–1½ hours, depending on the size of the potato. Cut across the top and scoop out the potato without breaking the shell. Mash the potato with milk, butter and a little salt, put it back in the skins and cover with grated cheese. Return to the oven and bake for 15 minutes or until brown on top.

I went to a Chinese
     restaurant, to buy a loaf of
     bread.
He wrapped it up in a
     five-pound note
And this is what he said
Ee ii, ee ii, chickabye,
     chickabye,
Do me a favour,
Drop dead.

MEN AND WOMEN IN THE KITCHEN

TO PRESERVE HUSBANDS

Husbands, like peaches, will not keep the year round unless they are well preserved.

Husbands grown in the tropics of pleasure look very fine, but are usually insipid. The home-grown are best. Select your husband, if possible, from a family tree, growing on the sunny side of a church. You will be sure then that he is sound at heart. Unsound husbands, like unsound peaches, often have to be sorrowfully cast away.

and . . .

HOLBROOKS

SWEET MUSTARD SAUCE

sweet . . . not hot!

Baby boomers were brought up with a number of assumptions about sexual characteristics. These had nothing to do with physiological differences of which we were profoundly ignorant. However, we all knew that men were useless in the kitchen, useless at shopping and, sadly, didn't really know what life was about.

Our fathers, on the other hand, conveyed the information that women were always fussing about in the kitchen, bought a lot of unnecessary things and didn't really know what life was about.

Our fathers went to work to earn the money. Our mothers stayed home to look after us and to cook and clean. The "opposite sex" was a very appropriate term. Our parents coped with it by making separate lives and disparaging jokes about each other.

Baby boomers remember their mothers in the kitchen. It is our most common image of them. Dads, on the other hand, only came into the kitchen to eat, to grab a beer or to be shooed out, like kids, for pinching a piece of cake or a sandwich.

Some men made successful forays into the kitchen. They might carve the roast, make the gravy, even cook a Sunday night tea to give their wives a night off. With massive culinary operations like bottling fruit or vegetables, it was often the men who had the expertise. That was scientific, it needed an expert, so it ceased to be women's work.

My grandmother used to send my grandfather out shopping. Inevitably, he would buy the wrong thing or too much of it or not enough. They both got enormous pleasure out of the exercise. "That's men for you . . . that's women for you."

Men might be called upon to wash up or dry up. But a man in an apron was a figure of fun, the henpecked husband of the cartoons that no real man would be.

However, men were arbiters of food quality. One baby boomer recalls how his father insisted the mashed potatoes be well mashed — he didn't like them with lumps. His mother promptly mashed them, with lots of milk, and poured them over his head. It may seem like an ordinary "domestic", but a point of honour was at stake.

HOW TO COOK HUSBANDS

A great many husbands are spoiled by mismanagement. Some women go about as if their husbands were bladders, and blow them up; others let them freeze by their carelessness and indifference. Some keep them in a stew, by irritating ways and words; others roast them; some keep them in pickle all their lives.

In selecting your husband you should not be guided by the silvery appearance as in buying mackerel, or by the golden tint as if you wanted salmon. Be sure to select him yourself, as tastes differ. And by the way, don't go to market for him, as the best are always brought to your door.

When properly treated they are really delicious.

The burnt chop syndrome existed in even the most blissful marriage. Dad got the best chop and Mum got the worst. That was the general order of things, never mind that Mum had cooked the food.

The Aussie male's robust sensibilities didn't allow him to enjoy fancy foods. Cookbooks and magazines advised women trying new recipes to present them with minimal fuss for fear of arousing male ire. And, of course, they shouldn't be too delicate. No "cuisine nouvelle" for our blokes, thank you.

CORN FRITTERS

A humble but wonderful recipe and one where the tinned ingredient does a better job than the fresh vegetable.

Ingredients

1 × 130 g (4 oz) tin sweetcorn or creamed corn

120 g (4 oz) self-raising flour

60 g (2 oz) cornflour

1 tablespoon oil

1 cup soda water

1 egg white

extra oil

parsley for garnish

Method

Beat the egg white until it is stiff. Mix the flour and cornflour, then add the oils and the soda water to form a smooth batter. Stir in the egg white, then the corn.

Heat a frypan with a little oil. Pour in tablespoonsful of the batter. Cook quickly on each side until golden brown. Drain on kitchen paper and serve hot with parsley.

MEAT FRITTERS

This is a quick and tasty way to use up the cold meat.

Ingredients

cold lamb or beef

120 g (4 oz) plain flour

1 egg

¾ cup milk

oil

Serves 6

Method

Chop the meat into small pieces. Mix the flour, the egg and the milk into a smooth batter. Add the meat. Spoon tablespoonsful of the batter into the frypan, one at a time. Have the frypan hot, with just a little oil. Fritters are cooked when they are brown on each side.

SCOTCH EGGS

The cholesterol-conscious will not want to eat this regularly. However, it is wonderfully comforting and a truly nostalgic food.

Ingredients

500 g (1 lb) sausage meat

6 hardboiled eggs

1 raw egg

breadcrumbs

oil

parsley for garnish

Serves 6

Method

Divide the sausage meat into 6 portions. Shell the hardboiled eggs. Place an egg on each portion and mould the sausage meat around the egg, keeping the egg shape. Beat the remaining egg. Dip each Scotch egg into it, then roll in breadcrumbs.

Heat the oil in a deep pan and place three of the eggs in a frying basket. They should not touch or they will stick together. When the oil is hot, fry the eggs until brown. Fry the other three. Cut each egg in half lengthways and serve immediately, garnished with parsley.

SECTION **G**

More about Eggs

A few drops of vinegar added to the water in which you are going to poach eggs will help to prevent them spreading.

Here's a simple way to separate the yolk from the white of an egg. Simply crack the egg into a funnel. The white will run through, the yolk will remain in the funnel.

WHITE WINGS Self Raising FLOUR.
One bake will PROVE it's better!

EGGS IN TOMATOES

This dish stands on its own. However, it also makes an excellent accompaniment to fish.

Ingredients

4 large tomatoes — ripe but still firm, and flat on the base

4 eggs

salt and pepper

chives

1 tablespoon crisp breadcrumbs

1 tablespoon parmesan cheese

Serves 4

Method

Slice the tops off the tomatoes. With a teaspoon, carefully scrape out the seeds and pulp, but leave the shells intact.

Beat the eggs, add a dash of salt and pepper and finely chopped chives, and pour them into the tomatoes. Combine the breadcrumbs and the parmesan cheese and sprinkle over the top. Place in a well-greased pie dish and bake in a moderate oven for about 30 minutes.

Wash the dishes, dry the
  dishes,
Turn the dishes over.

BACON AND EGG PIE

The French did some fancy things to this and called it
quiche. This one is for real baby boomers, although it is
not the pastry version many baby boomers will fondly
recall.

Ingredients

120 g (4 oz) bacon pieces

1 large onion

4 large eggs

1 large tomato thinly sliced

½ cup breadcrumbs

1 cup grated tasty cheese

Serves 6

Method

Slice the onion finely and fry up with the bacon pieces
until well cooked. Beat the eggs and pour into an ovenproof glass casserole. Gently arrange the slices of tomato
over the egg, then sprinkle with bacon, breadcrumbs and
finally the cheese. Bake at 220°C (425°F) for 15 minutes.

Gran's train gets in at 8.30

. . . and little Frances Kennedy and her mother of Penshurst, N.S.W., are hurrying off to meet her. So breakfast was a brisk affair this morning — the washing up even brisker !

But how lovely for Mrs. Kennedy when she gets back from the station, to see clean, gleaming dishes, and shining silver, all ready to put away.

"What a blessing New Rinso is !" she says. "There's nothing like those richer, softer suds for getting dishes done quickly. And how well Rinso looks after my hands !

"I get good value for my money with New Rinso, too. The suds never die down half-way through — they stay thick and busy till the last pan's shining !"

Whatever your reason for finishing sooner . . .

You'll wash up quicker and easier with NEW RINSO's richer, softer suds

JELLIED CHICKEN

This looks very, very 1950s. It's the peas, carrots and hardboiled eggs that do it.

This is a fairly straightforward recipe, but be warned — it does take time. It looks great and is an excellent summer dish. For the cholesterol-conscious, the hardboiled eggyolks may be omitted.

Ingredients

1 number 12 chicken

water

1 small bag mixed herbs

3 small cooked carrots

3 dessertspoons gelatine

2 hardboiled eggs

1 cup cooked peas

1 L (1¾ pints) water

salt, pepper

Romaine lettuce

Bread and butter, marmalade
  jam,
Tell me the name of your
  young man.

Serves 6–8

Method

Joint the chicken, place it in a saucepan with water and
bring to the boil. Cover the saucepan and boil for 1 hour
with the bag of herbs. Separate the chicken from the
broth. Remove herbs, and skim fat and waste from the
broth.

Dice up the chicken and cut the carrots into rings. Do
not proceed to the next stage until the chicken, the broth
and the vegetables are cool.

Heat a little of the broth and dissolve the gelatine in it.
Add this to the rest of the broth and mix in well.

Using an oblong mould, pour in a layer of broth. Put
this in the fridge and allow to set. Cut the hardboiled eggs
in half lengthways, remove the half yolks (intact) and
arrange them on the mould. Arrange in a pattern the
slices of egg white. Pour in some more broth and, when
almost set, arrange chicken and peas tastefully. You do
not have to wait for this to set before pouring on more
broth. Arrange a layer of carrots and chicken. Keep
adding layers, making full use of boomer artistry and
imagination. Make sure you have a layer of broth to finish
with. Allow to set.

Line the rim of a plate with Romaine lettuce. Unmould
the chicken by dipping it quickly into hot water and
rapping the sides sharply on sides and ends. Turn it out
onto the plate.

An Electric Clock is a necessity—
Accurate timing ensures well-cooked dishes.

Fried bananas

Traditionally, this dish was served with sausages. However, I can safely say that it stands well on its own — in fact, the sausages are best forgotten. The bananas can be served as a snack or as a dessert, with icecream or cream (or both!). If you really want to prove you have shed your baby boomer culinary past, add a dash of rum to the cream.

Ingredients

4 ripe bananas

plain flour

1 beaten egg

dried breadcrumbs

butter and oil

icing sugar

Method

Cut each banana lengthwise and then crosswise. Lightly coat each piece of banana in flour, dip it into the beaten egg, then roll in breadcrumbs. Fry in a mixture of half oil, half butter until brown on each side. Dust lightly with icing sugar before serving.

APPLE AND SULTANA PANCAKES

A great variation on the plain pancake with lemon and sugar.

Ingredients

60 g (2 oz) self-raising flour

60 g (2 oz) plain flour

60 g (2 oz) cornflour

30 g (1 oz) melted butter

1 cup soda water

1 egg yolk

2 stiffly beaten egg whites

½ can pie apple or an equal quantity of lightly stewed apples

40 g (1.3 oz) sultanas

oil and butter for frying

cinnamon and caster sugar

Serves 6

Method

Combine the flours. Pour in the melted butter, the soda water and the egg yolk. Mix well and then fold in the egg whites. Add the apples and the sultanas. Heat the butter and oil mixture and drop in the batter in spoonfuls. Cook until golden brown on both sides. Sprinkle with cinnamon and sugar and serve hot with icecream.

After television became part of our lives, Sunday night meant sitting around in dressing-gowns watching Disneyland.

I remember our first take-away. It was on Sunday night. We took a saucepan down to the Chinese restaurant. They filled it up with this shock orange stuff called sweet and sour pork. It was full of peas and bits of pineapple. We thought it was wonderful.

Dad cooked tea on Sunday nights. There was always a lot of tension, with Mum hovering in the background, waiting for him to do something disastrous.

Mum used to soak the leftover rice in the leftover tomato soup and cook it in a jaffle iron. That was real culinary creativity in the fifties.

We were supposed to have meat fritters from the leftover roast. But if it was a good enough roast, there wouldn't be any leftovers.

Sometimes we had tripe in batter. My brother used to make us sick by giving a vivid description of where it came from.

I only liked the brown bit on the bubble and squeak. But Mum wouldn't let me leave the insides.

Sunday nights! You didn't have to eat up the vegies to get pud!

In winter, we had tea round the heater. I had to sit nearest because Mum put my hair in rags to make it curly for the week and it had to be dry before we went to bed.

In summer we'd go down to the beach and have a picnic instead of having tea at home. We'd race in and out of the surf, grabbing a boiled egg or a sandwich, while Mum and the aunties had endless cups of tea out of the thermos.

Baby boomers in the kitchen

Our family moved into a house with a modern kitchen when I was six years old. It had a transfer of a sleeping Mexican on the wall, which I thought was wonderful. My mother insisted he be painted over, but he kept showing through numerous layers of paint, in a ghostly fashion.

We also had something called a "round and round". I find it hard to believe now, but this modern wonder was simply a curved bench, topped by some curved cupboards and shelves.

We also had a built-in table, which was too small to accommodate a whole baby booming family, but was nevertheless impressive. It had a built-in seat, with a special box to store your newspapers. The bench tops were of red Formica and the cupboards were green with red handles. Bright was the selling point. Bright it was.

The old-fashioned kitchen I remember best is my grandmother's, which was huge compared to our modern red and green kitchen. It had a big wooden table in the centre, with various non-matching chairs. My grandmother made pastry, cut up the meat and rolled out biscuits on the table. We ate there too. She had some glass-fronted cupboards on the wall, a pantry cupboard and a separate scullery. There was a safe and a kerosene fridge, but the dominating feature of her kitchen was the wood stove. It was lit first thing in the morning and stayed alight till late at night.

My grandmother's kitchen was big enough to allow the whole family to sit down in comfort, but it wasn't modern.

In the 1950s and 60s "modern" meant Laminex, rainbow walls, vinyl floors and an electric range and an electric fridge. It meant gadgets, like knife-racks and spice-racks and peg-boards. It meant having a filing-box for your recipes and plastic canisters instead of the old tin ones. "Modern" could also be incredibly ugly and far too small. With post-war building regulations, it was hard to get past the box-like structures beloved by government authorities.

There was a brave, new, plastic world feel to it. Everything was easy-wipe and easy-clean. Perhaps because domestic service had become a thing of the past, women wanted things small and easy to look after.

Understandably, they didn't want to worry with safes and icechests and chopping wood. Perhaps the garish colours and the Mexicans on the wall were their way of showing that they had left the Depression, the war and wood stoves behind them.

Twenty years later, their children, the baby boomers, had become hippies and flower children. They were putting flowerpots in their kitchen, painting them orange and purple, and bemoaning the fact that the world no longer gave them an opportunity to chop wood or draw water.

6 CAKES

Cake-making was something that baby boomers' mothers spent a lot of time doing. Packet cakes and shop-bought cakes might make an occasional appearance, but the Aussie mums of the 1940s, 50s and 60s regarded home-made cake as an essential part of the diet. Of course, children weren't supposed to have too much cake, but cake did contain butter and eggs, and they were supposed to be good for you.

LAMINGTONS

No baby boomers' cookbook would be complete without a lamington recipe. However, I confess I have never success-fully made a lamington. My attempts end up with me and my lamingtons looking as if we have been engaged in mortal combat. A successful lamington-maker rather briskly assured me the following method is *fool* proof. Be a *real* baby boomer. Try it.

Ingredients

240 g (8 oz) butter

360 g (11 oz) sugar

4 eggs

3 cups self-raising flour

1 cup milk

1 teaspoon vanilla essence

Icing

240 g (8 oz) icing sugar mixture

2 dessertspoons cocoa

2 tablespoons water

1 cup desiccated coconut

Method

Cream the butter and sugar. Add the eggs, then the flour, and finally the milk, with the vanilla. Bake in a square tin at 180°C (350°F) for about 25 minutes.

Mix the icing sugar, cocoa and water to such a consistency that the icing just runs. When the cake is cold, cut it into squares. Hold a square of cake on a fork and coat each side with icing, using a knife to spread it. Put the coconut onto a large plate and dip each side into the coconut.

Cakes were mother love.

ORANGE CAKE

Baby boomer mothers made this as an afternoon tea cake. Wrapped in greaseproof paper and stored in a tin, it lasted the week.

Ingredients

120 g (4 oz) butter

120 g (4 oz) sugar

3 eggs

grated rind of 2 small oranges

2 cups self-raising flour

½ cup milk

Icing

1 cup icing sugar

1 tablespoon orange juice

1 teaspoon butter, melted

water if needed

Method

Cream the butter and sugar. Beat in the eggs one at a time. Add the grated orange rind, then the flour and milk alternately. Make sure the ingredients are thoroughly mixed.

Put into two sandwich tins or one large square tin. Bake in a moderate oven for about 25 minutes.

Combine the icing sugar, juice and melted butter. Add water if necessary but keep the icing stiff. Ice the cake when cold.

Whenever I smell a chocolate cake, I think of my mother.

SWISS ROLL

This is very different from the often dreary cake shop variety. Light and fluffy and especially good with a slightly sour jam, such as sour cherry.

Ingredients

3 eggs

1 pinch salt

120 g (4 oz) sugar

120 g (4 oz) self-raising flour

3 tablespoons milk

extra caster sugar

1 cup raspberry jam

Method

Separate egg whites from yolks. Beat whites with salt until they form stiff peaks. Add the sugar very gradually, beating to maintain the stiffness of the mixture. Add the yolks one at a time and stir in gently. Sift the flour into the mixture and gently fold it through. (The aim is to

keep as much air in the mixture as possible. Add the milk. Bake at 220°C (425°F) for 8–10 minutes in a lightly greased Swiss roll tin.

While the sponge is cooking, sprinkle the extra sugar over a piece of greaseproof paper slightly larger than the cake. When the cake is cooked, turn the sponge onto the greaseproof paper. Spread the jam over it and roll it lengthways. When cool, serve with cream.

BUTTERFLY CAKES

These always intrigued me as a child, as I seemed to get them only at parties. I am pleased to have learnt at last how to make the butterfly.

Ingredients

30 g (1 oz) butter

60 g (2 oz) sugar

People didn't think they were bad for you. Anyway, it was only ever one slice each.

1 egg
90 g (3 oz) self-raising flour
1 tablespoon milk
lemon butter (see below)
whipped cream
icing sugar
10 patty cases

Method

Cream the butter and sugar. Add the egg, flour and milk, beating well.

Bake in a moderate oven at 180°C (350°F) in 10 patty cases for 10–15 minutes.

When cold, remove from the patty cases. Slice the top off each cake and cut this top in half. Spread each cake first with lemon butter, then cream. Then arrange the two cut pieces — the wings — in the cream. Sprinkle with icing sugar.

Lemon butter

Everyone used to have a jar of this in their pantry. Now you can buy it in the supermarket, but it's easy to make yourself.

Ingredients

3 dessertspoons butter
150 g (5 oz) sugar
grated rind and juice of 1 lemon
2 eggs

Method

Melt the butter in the top half of a double saucepan. Add the sugar and the lemon rind and juice. Beat the eggs and add to the other ingredients. Cook over boiling water, stirring all the time until the mixture thickens. Use cold as a filling.

SPONGE CAKE

In my childhood, the making of a sponge spelled emotional crisis. Sponges failed to rise, listed to one side or fell before the very eyes of the guests. In the 1950s the sponge was more than a cake. It was proof of true womanhood. Try it if you dare.

Ingredients

6 × 55 g (1¾ oz) eggs

240 g (8 oz) sugar

3 tablespoons water

a few drops of vanilla

240 g (8 oz) plain flour

1 pinch salt

Method

Preheat the oven to 250°C (500°F) (hot). Grease a sponge tin and sprinkle it very lightly with sifted flour.

Boil the sugar and water together for 1 minute. Break the eggs into a basin and pour the sugar and water slowly over them. Beat well, until thick. Add the essence, then stir in the flour and salt. Quickly transfer the mixture to the tin and then to the oven. After a few minutes reduce the temperature to 180°C (350°F) (slow) and cook for 1 hour. Turn out onto a wire rack.

When cool, fill with lemon butter or jam and cream. Sprinkle with icing sugar.

CAUSES OF FAILURE IN CAKE MAKING

Careless measurement of ingredients, which is responsible for:—
Incorrect proportions of ingredients.
Wrong consistency of mixture.
Insufficient beating of butter, sugar and eggs.
Too much stirring after the addition of flour and baking powder.
Damp fruit.
Incorrect heat of oven and heat control.
Opening oven door too soon or too frequently.
Slamming oven door.

Rain, rain go away,
come again another day.
When I brew and when I bake,
I'll make you a Johnny cake.

TEACAKE

Compared to a sponge, this cake is a breeze and virtually idiot-proof.

Ingredients

1 tablespoon butter

1 tablespoon sugar

1 egg

½ cup milk

1 cup self-raising flour

Topping

1 teaspoon butter

1 teaspoon cinnamon

2 tablespoons caster sugar

Method

Cream the butter and sugar. Add the egg, then the milk and the flour. Beat until smooth. Pour into a greased tin and bake at 200°C (390°F) for 15–20 minutes.

Turn out onto a wire rack. Butter the top of the cake. Combine the cinnamon and sugar and sprinkle over evenly. Eat while hot, with a cuppa.

GINGERBREAD

Now a much neglected cake. Great for picnics.

Ingredients

3 cups self-raising flour

1 tablespoon ground ginger

60 g (2 oz) butter

2 eggs

1 cup milk

½ cup sugar

1 cup treacle

Method

Combine the flour and the ginger. Rub the butter through the flour till the mixture has a crumbly texture. Beat the eggs. Add the milk, the sugar and then the treacle. Add the flour mixture and beat well. Grease a shallow tin and pour in the mixture. Bake at 180°C (350°F) for 30–45 minutes. Allow to cool in the tin and then cut into squares.

Patty cake, patty cake,
baker's man.
Bake me a cake,
as fast as you can.
Pat it and prick it,
and mark it with T.
Put it in the oven,
for Tommy and me!

GINGER SPONGE

A very traditional baby boomer cake. Make sure you have your sponge sandwich tins to cook it in.

Ingredients

120 g (4 oz) butter

1 cup sugar

2 eggs

½ cup golden syrup

1½ cups self-raising flour

1 teaspoon mixed spice

1 teaspoon ginger

1 pinch nutmeg

½ cup milk

1 teaspoon bicarbonate of soda

Method

Cream butter and sugar. Add the eggs, then the syrup, then the flour, together with the spices, ginger and nutmeg. Last, add the milk in which the soda has been dissolved. Bake in two sandwich tins at 180°C (350°F) for 25 minutes. Join with lemon icing. Sprinkle the top with icing sugar. Excellent as a cake or with pears and icecream for dessert.

MARBLE CAKE

This is a cake that appeals to small minds. Well, mine at least. I just love the way it looks. Top it with marbled pink and chocolate icing.

Ingredients

240 g (8 oz) butter

240 g (8 oz) sugar

3 eggs separated

250 mL (8 fl oz) milk

500 g (1 lb) self-raising flour

1 pinch salt

vanilla essence

2 teaspoons cocoa

pink food colouring

Method

Cream the butter and sugar. Add the egg yolks and beat well. Add the milk, flour, salt and vanilla. Beat the egg whites until very stiff and fold into the mixture.

Divide the mixture into three separate bowls. Add the cocoa to one bowl and the pink colouring to another. Keep the colouring subtle. Grease a deep square tin or a large oblong one. Put in half the plain mixture. Top with the pink mix and then the chocolate one. Top off with the remaining plain mixture. Fork it through gently two or three times. Don't overdo the mixing or you'll simply get an insipid fawn cake. Let the oven do it for you. Bake at 180°C (350°F) for about 90 minutes.

FUDGE CAKE

This is a cake I loved to make when I was a kid. It's simple, foolproof and deliciously chocolatey. Great for a winter afternoon tea, but don't use it when you want to appear incredibly sophisticated.

Ingredients

1 cup sugar

2 tablespoons cocoa

60 g (2 oz) butter or margarine

1 egg

1 pinch salt

1½ cups self-raising flour

½ cup milk

Method

Mix the sugar and cocoa. Add the melted butter or margarine. Beat the egg and add it to the mixture with the salt. Then add the flour and milk. Bake in patty tins or a single round tin at 180°C (350°F) for 15 minutes.

SIGNS THAT CAKES ARE COOKED

SPONGES: Shrink from sides of tin and are elastic to the touch.
SMALL CAKES: Elastic to the touch.
LARGE CAKES: A skewer placed in the thickest part comes out clean.

CHOCOLATE BISCUIT CAKE
(See recipe opposite page)

ROCK CAKES

These cakes were used as fillers for baby boomer kids. Guaranteed as a substantial afternoon tea.

Ingredients

240 g (8 oz) plain flour

1 tablespoon baking powder

90 g (3 oz) butter

90 g (3 oz) sugar

1 tablespoon finely chopped dates

1 tablespoon currants

1 egg

½ cup milk

Method

Mix the flour and the baking powder and rub in the butter lightly. Add the sugar, dates and currants. Mix the milk and the egg well, and add to the mixture. Grease an oven slide and put heaped dessertspoons of the mixture onto the slide. Bake at 220°C (425°F) for 10–15 minutes. Serve when cold.

BAKING CAKES

For the best results, including perfection in the browning of cakes, have the oven heated to the correct temperature before placing cakes in to cook, and cook with a gradually decreasing heat.

Avoid placing rich fruit cakes in too hot an oven. The great heat cooks and hardens the outside before the heat has reached the centre of the cake, retarding the rising and preventing even cooking throughout the cake.

SAND CAKE

This cake was usually made and served by grandmothers at afternoon tea, after a spirited game of bridge. The best the baby boomer grandchildren could hope for on such a day was a slice of cake — a reward for "being good".

Ingredients

240 g (8 oz) butter

240 g (8 oz) sugar

4 eggs

240 g (8 oz) arrowroot

Method

Cream the butter and sugar. Add the eggs one at a time, beating thoroughly. Add the arrowroot and mix in well. Grease a square cake tin. Spoon in the mixture and bake in a slow oven for 45 minutes.

UPSIDE-DOWN CAKE

Another one of those magic recipes. A very impressive-looking cake if you grease the tin *thoroughly*, so the cake turns out with the topping intact.

Ingredients

90 g (3 oz) butter or margarine

240 g (8 oz) sugar

2 eggs

270 g (9 oz) self-raising flour

¾ cup milk

1 teaspoon vanilla

Topping

3 heaped tablespoons brown sugar

90 g (3 oz) butter

1 tin drained pineapple pieces

Method

Cream the butter and sugar for the topping and spread on the bottom of a lightly greased square cake tin. Arrange the pineapple pieces over the butter and sugar.

Cream the butter and sugar for the cake. Beat in the eggs. Add the flour, milk and vanilla and beat well. Spoon it carefully over the pineapple.

Bake at 180°C (350°F) for 35 minutes. Allow to rest for 15 minutes, then turn carefully onto the serving plate.

MOCK CREAM FILLING

- 1 tblsp. Butter
- 1 tblsp. Castor Sugar
- 1 tblsp. boiling Water
- 1 tblsp. Milk
- ¼ tsp. Vanilla

METHOD: Beat butter and sugar until sugar is completely dissolved. Add boiling water, a drop at a time, then milk, a drop at a time. Finally, add the vanilla essence. (This is an excellent soft, creamy-textured filling.)

COPYRIGHT

COCONUT CAKE

Some baby boomers still believe that desiccated coconut gives you polio. Not true! Remember, we all had our shots anyway.

Ingredients

120 g (4 oz) butter or margarine

¾ cup caster sugar

2 eggs

finely grated rind of ½ lemon

1 teaspoon vanilla

1½ cups self-raising flour

½ cup milk

½ cup desiccated coconut

Icing

1 level tablespoon margarine

2 tablespoons boiling water

1 teaspoon lemon juice

a few drops of vanilla essence

1½ cups icing sugar mixture

½ cup desiccated coconut

milk to moisten if necessary

Method

Cream butter and sugar, then gradually beat in the eggs one at a time. Add lemon rind and vanilla. Add flour and milk gradually, beating well. Finally, add the coconut.

Pour into a greased loaf tin and bake for about 45 minutes at 180°C (350°F). When cool, top with the icing.

For the icing, melt the margarine in the boiling water and add the lemon juice and vanilla. Add icing sugar mix and coconut, and milk if necessary. However, the icing is best kept fairly stiff.

Coconut Cake

Follow Basic 2 egg recipe, but:
1. Add 3 ozs. coconut with the second addition of flour.
2. Bake in a greased and floured loaf pan (9 x 4 x 2½") in a moderate oven, 350°F. gas, 50-55 minutes. A tin 9 x 9 x 2" may be used, baking for 35 minutes.
3. Frost, when cool, with Coconut Ice Frosting (see recipe Frostings Section).

PAGE 7

EUROPEAN JAM CRESCENTS

The word European spelt sophistication to the baby boomer. Remember European clothes, European hairstyles — passport to that *je ne sais quoi*. In a modest way, these European jam crescents transcend red-brick suburbia.

Ingredients

180 g (6 oz) margarine

180 g (6 oz) plain flour

180 g (6 oz) spreadable cream cheese

¾ cup raspberry jam

a little beaten egg white

caster sugar

icing sugar

Method

Cut the margarine into the flour, then rub it in lightly. Mix to a dough with the cream cheese. Chill for 30 minutes. Roll out to 2 mm (⅛ in) thickness. Cut into squares about 8 cm (3 in). Spread with jam to 1 cm (⅓ in) of each edge. Starting in one corner, roll to the opposite corner, so that you finish up with the corner on top. Pull the ends round a bit, to form a crescent. Brush lightly with beaten egg white and sprinkle lightly with caster sugar. Put on a greased oven slide, with space between the crescents, and bake at 180°C (350°F) for 25 minutes. Dust with icing sugar before serving.

Coming home from school and seeing a cake just out of the oven — it used to drive me mad when we had to wait for them to cool.

Mum would bake a cake for Sunday afternoon tea. Then it would be wrapped in greaseproof paper and put in a tin. There would be a slice a day after school until it ran out. After that, it was Anzacs for the rest of the week.

Learning to cook in our house started with learning to make cakes. Not terribly healthy, but great fun.

We loved coming in after the grownups had finished their afternoon tea. We had the leftovers, but we thought it was great.

The best bit about Mum making a cake was to be allowed to lick the spoon and the bowl.

CHILDREN'S FOOD

Out of the mouths of babes and sucklings . . .

We had our baths, had our tea and were put to bed by seven. We didn't eat with our parents until we were ten or eleven.

The baby's food was a bit of a drama. Mum would cook his vegetables forever, then put them through a sieve. She'd put his bib on and have the food at just the right temperature. She'd shovel it in and he'd spit it out. No wonder she was angry.

For morning tea, we always had sliced banana with milk and sugar. When you were five, you got an arrowroot biscuit instead.

Blancmange: chocolate, vanilla or strawberry, they all tasted the same. I just hated it.

We kids had junket for tea on Sunday nights. Junket! It was supposed to be good for our digestion.

Brains were supposed to be good for children, but our parents never ate them.

Mum used to give us stewed chops. I can still remember the smell.

We often had eggs for tea. Poached on Vegemite toast.

Straight fish was too strong for children, so we had fish cakes. Basically, they were mashed up potato with fish, fried in breadcrumbs. Enough to put you off fish for life.

White sauce was the bane of my life — brains in white sauce, tripe in white sauce, fish in white sauce. I think it was supposed to be a gentle introduction to various revolting foods.

I was a delicate child, but I couldn't have been all that delicate because I survived all my mother's remedies. Arrowroot broth, molasses in hot water and beef tea.

Mum used to make us lemonade. She'd squeeze a lemon, add a few spoonfuls of sugar and mix it up with hot water. We'd wait till it cooled. Back then, it tasted all right, which I guess said something about the rest of our food.

The best children's food was baked apple. Mum used to sprinkle icing sugar over it. The grownups never got them in our house.

We used to get bread and milk. Mum cut up the bread, heated up the milk and poured it over and then sprinkled sugar over it. I thought it was great until I was about five.

7 BIKKIES AND SCONES

B.B. biscuits are the best,
When you eat them, they digest.
With a north, south, east and west.

A proper afternoon tea, the sort our mothers and grand-mothers put on for their friends, usually involved several cakes and different types of home-made biscuits.

Biscuits were also very much children's food — a couple of biscuits in your pocket riding your bike, some nicked from the biscuit tin when your mother was out, biscuits with billy tea at family picnics.

ANZACS

The Anzac biscuit has become a symbol of the baby boomer childhood. Depending on the cook, Anzacs come in many guises — crisp, soggy, pliable and crumbly — all with their own particular charm.

Ingredients

1½ cups rolled oats

2 tablespoons golden syrup

110 g (3¾ oz) butter

2 teaspoons bicarbonate of soda

1 cup self-raising flour

1 cup desiccated coconut

1 cup sugar

1 pinch salt

1 egg

Mum made the Anzacs on a Tuesday. I still remember the smell of hot Anzac biscuits.

Method

Heat the golden syrup, butter and baking soda, then stir in the oats, flour and coconut. Add the sugar and the salt.

Finally, add the egg. Knead well. Pinch off small balls, flatten slightly and place on a greased baking tray. Leave room for the biscuits to spread.

Cook at 180°C (350°F) for 15–20 minutes. The biscuits are cooked when golden brown.

GINGERNUTS

A hearty, tasty biscuit and dead easy to make.

Ingredients

240 g (8 oz) plain flour

1 pinch salt

1 slightly heaped dessertspoon powdered ginger

60 g (2 oz) brown sugar

1 teaspoon bicarbonate of soda

2 tablespoons milk

2 tablespoons treacle

60 g (2 oz) butter or margarine

Method

Heat the oven at 180°C (350°F) and grease a biscuit slide. Mix the flour, salt, ginger and sugar together in a bowl. Mix the baking soda into the milk. Melt the treacle and the butter and add to the milk. Mix with the dry ingredients to form a dough. Mould the dough into a ball and roll it out, on a floured board, to a thickness of about 5 mm (⅙ in). Cut out with an eggcup or a round biscuit cutter. Place on a greased biscuit slide and cook for about 10 minutes.

Nicking biscuits — crime and punishment. It took up an awful lot of my childhood.

Cooking was for girls. But when I was sick, my mother made biscuit dough and I'd cut it out with specially shaped cutters.

VANILLA BISCUITS

Compared to the hearty Anzac, the vanilla biscuit is more delicate and refined. As my mother used to say, it won't spoil your dinner.

Ingredients

60 g (2 oz) butter

60 g (2 oz) sugar

1 egg yolk

a dash of vanilla

120 g (4 oz) self-raising flour

1 egg white

blanched almonds

Method

Heat the oven at a moderate setting and prepare a greased biscuit slide. Cream the butter and sugar. Add the eggyolk and beat well. Add the vanilla, then the flour. Lightly mix to a dough, roll it out thinly on a floured board, and cut with a floured biscuit cutter. Place on the greased slide and glaze lightly with the eggwhite. Put half an almond on each. Bake for 10 minutes, or until they turn a delicate brown.

There was a hierarchy of biscuit tins — the old scratched one for the savoury stuff, right up to the one with the picture of the Coronation for the visitors' biscuits.

OATMEAL SHORTBREAD

Shortbread was traditionally served at Christmas time — usually a definite overkill by the time the chook, the pudding, mince pies and cakes had been served. Shortbread, particularly this delicious oatmeal version, has always seemed an appropriate treat for cold winter afternoons.

Ingredients

1½ cups butter or margarine

¾ cup caster sugar

2 cups porridge oats

2 cups self-raising flour

1 pinch salt

Method

Cream the butter and the sugar. Gradually add the oats, flour and salt. Knead until it forms a very smooth dough. Divide into four equal portions. Fashion each of these into a round cake a little over 1 cm (⅓ in) thick. Pinch around the edges and prick the surface with a fork. Bake at 160°C (320°F) on a lightly greased slide for 30–40 minutes. Leave on the trays until cold. Shortbread must be stored in airtight containers.

BRAN BISCUITS

Our ancestors weren't too keen on natural bran. They preferred to have anything with laxative properties straight out of a bottle. These delicious bran biscuits are an exception.

Ingredients

60 g (2 oz) butter

2 tablespoons brown sugar

1 egg

½ cup milk

1 cup self-raising flour

1 cup bran

1 pinch salt

Method

Cream the butter and the sugar. Add the egg and the milk. Add the dry ingredients and mix well to form a dough. Roll out thinly on a floured board. Bake at 220°C (425°F) for 20 minutes.

We always had to eat the burnt ones. Mum never threw anything out.

Chocolate caramel slice

This is definitely a top-of-the-line, official afternoon tea biscuit. As a child, you probably only ate it when various aunts and other rels had had their share. Indulge yourself by making a whole batch.

Ingredients

The slice

1 cup self-raising flour

1 cup brown sugar

1 cup desiccated coconut

125 g (4 oz) melted margarine

1 egg

The caramel

400 g (12 oz) sweetened condensed milk

2 tablespoons golden syrup

30 g (1 oz) margarine

Chocolate topping

250 g (8 oz) cooking chocolate

30 g (1 oz) Copha (or margarine)

Method

Combine the ingredients for the slice and press into a greased lamington tin (approximately 20 x 25 cm or 8 x 10 in). Bake for 10 minutes at 180°C (350°F).

To make the caramel, combine the ingredients in a heavy saucepan. Bring to the boil and stir for 5 minutes as it gently simmers. Take care not to burn it.

When the slice is cool, pour the hot caramel onto it and bake it for another 10 minutes at 180°C (350°F).

When it has cooled a little, heat the chocolate and Copha and when they liquefy, pour them over. Put it in the refrigerator until chilled. Cut into small squares and serve.

COCONUT MACAROONS

These are dual-purpose biscuits. They are delicious on their own, but are also the basis for the summer dessert, marshmallow macaroons (see Summer puddings, Chapter 3). In our house, they never lasted long enough to make it to dessert.

Ingredients

2 egg whites

180 g (6 oz) caster sugar

90 g (3 oz) desiccated coconut

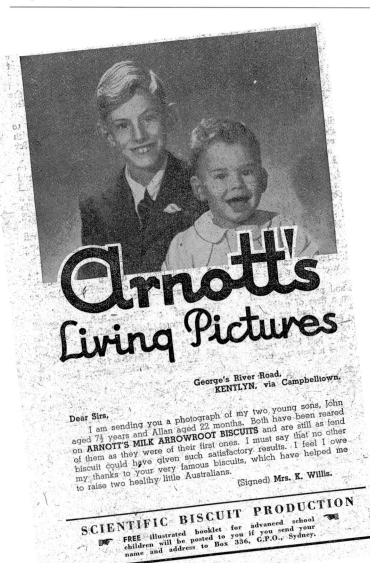

We used to long for bought biscuits. Now I long for homemade ones.

30 g (1 oz) ground rice

1 pinch salt

Method

Prepare a greased biscuit slide and heat the oven to 170°C (335°F). Beat the egg whites until they form very stiff peaks. Add half the sugar and beat until the mixture is very stiff. (It is vital to keep the egg white mixture stiff, otherwise the macaroons will be chewy and flat rather than crisp and pointed. Mind you, even the flat ones are quite pleasant.) Fold in the rest of the ingredients. With a dessertspoon, place blobs of the mixture onto the slide. Cook for 30 minutes. The biscuits should not brown.

BRANDYSNAPS

The fun part of this recipe, apart from eating the finished product, is rolling these into shape while the biscuit is still hot.

Ingredients

90 g (3 oz) butter

100 g (3½ oz) caster sugar

90 g (3 oz) golden syrup

100 g (3½ oz) flour

1 teaspoon brandy

1 pinch salt

1 teaspoon ground ginger

Method

Melt butter, sugar and golden syrup. Gradually mix in the flour, brandy, salt and ginger and stir well. Drop in small lumps onto a greased oven slide, leaving plenty of room for each one to spread. Bake in a moderate oven for 10 minutes. While still hot, wrap each one round the handle of a wooden spoon to form a tube. Take them off and allow to cool and harden. Serve filled with whipped cream.

My earliest memory of cooking is of helping to roll out the biscuits. Then I learned how to make some simple ones. By the age of eight, I could produce a very good batch of biscuits on my own.

WALNUT BISCUITS

These are really great and you can't buy them.

Ingredients

240 g (8 oz) butter

1 cup sugar

1 egg

1 cup chopped dates

1 cup chopped walnuts

2 cups plain flour

2 teaspoons cinnamon

1 pinch nutmeg

1 teaspoon bicarbonate of soda dissolved in a little water

Method

Cream the butter and sugar and add the egg. Beat well and add the dates and walnuts. Add the flour and spices and the bicarbonate of soda. Grease a biscuit slide and spoon the mixture onto it with a tablespoon. Bake at 200°C (400°F) for 20–25 minutes.

CARAMEL DATE BISCUITS

Another hearty biscuit good for picnics.

Ingredients

120 g (4 oz) butter

120 g (4 oz) brown sugar

1 egg

1 cup plain flour

2 cups chopped dates

Method

Cream the butter and brown sugar. Do not melt the butter, as the creamed mixture should be stiff. Add beaten egg, flour and dates and mix thoroughly.

Smooth into a lightly greased biscuit tin. Cook at 170°C (335°F) for 30 minutes.

Cut into fingers and remove from the tray while still warm. Leave to cool and harden on a wire rack. Store any leftovers in an airtight container.

SCONES

Scones hold a proud place in the Australian afternoon tea. The following is a small selection of the various types of scones I sampled in my childhood.

Plain scones

These are very easy, but for years mine came out of the oven the consistency of rocks. I've learnt the trick. When they say don't knead the dough, *don't knead the dough.*

Ingredients

1 tablespoon butter

2 cups self-raising flour

1 pinch salt

equal parts milk and water, mixed

Method

Rub the butter into the flour and salt. Add enough of the milk and water mixture to form a soft dough. This should be done slowly so that the dough does not become wet and sticky. Work quickly *without* kneading the dough. Place the dough on a lightly floured board and pat it out to a thickness of about 2.5 cm (1 in). The aim is to handle the dough as little as possible. Cut into shapes with a floured scone cutter or sharp knife. Place on a greased and floured scone tray and bake at 240°C (475°F) for 10–12 minutes. Serve with butter, or jam and cream.

Pumpkin scones

These may never be trendy, but Aunty Flo certainly made pumpkin scones famous.

Ingredients

1 cup well mashed cooked pumpkin

2 dessertspoons sugar

1 tablespoon margarine

1 egg

3 cups self-raising flour

Method

Warm the pumpkin, sugar and margarine gently in a saucepan, mixing well. Beat the egg and add to the pumpkin mix when it is cool. Add this to the flour and make into a dough. Roll out to 1 cm (⅓ in) thickness and cut into squares. Lay them out on a lightly floured oven slide so they are not touching. Cook at 225°C (430°F) for 10 minutes.

Ma's treacle scones

Ma goes back a few generations. The survival of the recipe is testimony to the wonder of this recipe.

Ingredients

2 heaped cups self-raising flour

½ cup sugar

1 heaped teaspoon ginger

1 tablespoon treacle stirred into ¼ cup boiling water

a little milk if necessary

Method

Combine all the ingredients into a dough and bake for about 10 minutes at 225°C (430°F).

Drop scones

The instant gratification scone, and great fun to make.

Ingredients

1 cup plain flour

1 dessertspoon sugar

1 teaspoon bicarbonate of soda

1 teaspoon cream of tartar

1 egg

¾ cup milk

Method

Mix the flour and the sugar and add the bicarbonate of soda and cream of tartar. Beat the egg, combine the milk with it, then pour this into the flour, to make a smooth batter. Rub butter lightly over a non-stick frypan. Allow it to get hot on the stove and drop in teaspoonsful of the mixture. As bubbles appear on the surface of each one, flip it over to cook the other side. The drop scone should be slightly browned. It can be served hot or cold with butter and jam.

Gem scones

For these, you need a gem iron, or a patty cake tray.

Ingredients

30 g (1 oz) butter

60 g (2 oz) sugar

1 egg

2 cups self-raising flour

1 cup milk

Method

Heat the oven and put in the gem scone tray. Cream the butter and sugar. Add the egg, beating well. Add the flour and the milk. Using a pastry brush or kitchen paper, grease the hot gem scone tray with butter. While it is still hot, spoon in the mixture, filling each about three-quarters full. Bake in a hot oven 10–12 minutes. Split open and butter or serve when cold.

Betty's date scones

Betty was a large lady who smelt of Herco hand-lotion and left a lipstick imprint on small children. The memory

of her date scones is even more vivid. Taste Betty's date scones and you'll stop hating dates.

Ingredients

1 egg

240 mL (8 fl oz) milk

30 g (1 oz) butter

240 g (8 oz) self-raising flour

150 g (5 oz) dates, pitted and chopped

3 tablespoons sugar

Method

Beat the egg and milk together. Rub the butter into the flour. Add dates and sugar, then the liquid. Mix into a dough and roll out on a lightly floured board to about 1.5 cm (½ in) thick. Cut into squares and bake in a moderate oven for 20 minutes.

DOMESTIC SCIENCE

We had to wear white caps and white overalls and we learned to fry sausages and make gravy. All to make us future wives and mothers.

I dipped out. But then I'd dropped out of sewing when I was seven, so it didn't surprise me. They thought I'd never be a proper woman.

I had notebooks filled with information on oven temperatures and the properties of self-raising flour. My grandmother, who was a great cook, used to look at it and snort.

We were allowed to eat what we cooked. In fact, we had to eat what we cooked.

My mother had never let me near the kitchen, so it was quite good for me. I learned how to make scones. I was very proud of that.

I loved cooking at home, so I thought I'd be great. But there was only one way to do things and that was the way of the domestic science mistress. I gave it up after the first year.

We had a domestic science excursion to the abattoirs. About half the class immediately became vegetarians.

"Why don't they teach you to wash up?" my mother used to ask. In fact they did, but I wasn't letting on.

All I remember of cooking lessons was writing an essay called "The organisation of the provisions cupboard" for which I got ten out of ten. You should see my cupboards now!

The boys did woodwork while we did cooking. At least we got something to eat. They only got a letter- rack to take home to their mothers at the end of term.

We had to know about *kitchen requisites, cookery terms*, the *ten most common garnishes* and the *table of measures*. We never actually cooked anything.

We couldn't cook anything because they hadn't built the school kitchens. We learnt how to cook everything, but we never actually did it. The teacher was lovely. She'd say "Try it at home, girls," but by the end of the year, she was a bit desperate.

8 CHRISTMAS FARE AND THE EASTER BUNNY

Christmas crackers, penny a packet,
when you light them, they go bang.
Easter crackers, tuppence a packet,
when you light them, they go bang.

Christmas, for children of the baby boomer era, meant new toys, Christmas trees and cutting out silver stars. It also meant Christmas dinner, the annual culinary triumph of mothers. That meant a rare taste of chicken, sixpences in the Christmas pudding, being allowed to have a shandy, and the remains of the ham into the New Year.

You had to order your chook from the butcher. If you didn't order early, you couldn't be sure of a good bird. It was that competitive.

DIRECTIONS FOR DRAWING AND TRUSSING POULTRY

1. Pluck and singe the bird.
2. Scald feet and legs. Remove nails and horny skin, and truss.
For Roasting.—*Break legs between foot and knee, then twist foot until the sinews are exposed. Draw out sinews with skewer. Leave leg on while cooking to prevent flesh from shrinking and exposing bone. After cooking cut off leg at knee. Press legs well against body of fowl and secure with string or skewer. Secure flap of skin left on neck with wings.*
Ducks and Geese.—*Leave feet on when trussing, and twist legs round the body in such a way that feet lie flat on the back. Remove tips of wings of ducks and geese before trussing.*
For Geese and Ducks *forcemeat is placed in the body of birds.*
For Fowls and Turkeys, *put forcemeat in neck.*
Boiled ham or grilled bacon should be served with poultry and game, as they lack fat.
Trussing for Boiling.—*Sever legs at knee joint, then loosen skin of leg so that the legs can be pressed back into the body.*
Boning Poultry.—*Birds should be undrawn when boned. Begin at back of bird and lift the flesh with a sharp knife from each side until the legs and wings are reached. Legs and wings should be severed from the body, but the bony carcass should be intact. Bone legs and wings separately.*

Xmas
1958

2LB. CAKE IN CARTON

3LB. CAKE IN TIN

Again Available...

Arnott's *famous*
Xmas Cakes

AND "ALPINE" GIFT TIN OF BISCUITS

There is no Substitute for Quality

CHRISTMAS CAKE

Some baby boomers allow extra amounts of all fruit and nuts. This allows the cook and others to sample the ingredients without too much guilt.

Ingredients

120 g (4 oz) almonds

360 g (11 oz) raisins

360 g (11 oz) sultanas

120 g (4 oz) glacé cherries

60 g (2 oz) dried apricots cut finely

60 g (2 oz) glacé pineapple cut finely

3 tablespoons brandy

3 tablespoons sherry

240 g (8 oz) butter

240 g (8 oz) brown sugar

1 lemon rind, grated

1 tablespoon golden syrup

2 tablespoons marmalade

300g (9½ oz) plain flour

5 eggs

1 teaspoon mixed spice

1 teaspoon cinnamon

¼ teaspoon salt

Method

Keep aside 30 g almonds to put on the top of the cake. Also keep aside 1 tablespoon of brandy and 1 tablespoon of sherry. Soak the fruit in the brandy and sherry overnight. Cream butter and sugar. Add the lemon rind, golden syrup, and marmalade. Beat well until well com-

Christmas meant Mum getting everything out of layby in November and the Christmas cake being cooked.

bined. Alternately add a little of the flour and one egg, beating well each time. Add the rest of the flour, then the spices, and finally the fruit, brandy and sherry mixture and the almonds.

Line a 20 cm (8 in) square tin with two layers of greased paper. Spoon in the mixture and arrange the remaining almonds over the top. Cook in a slow 150°C (300°F) oven for 3–4 hours. When cool, sprinkle extra brandy and sherry over the cake.

CHRISTMAS PUDDING

You can use butter or marge instead of suet, but purists will stick with the real thing.

Ingredients

150 g (5 oz) suet

500 g (1 lb) plain flour

6 eggs

500 g (1 lb) brown sugar

I loved the pudding being set on fire. Dad did it every year with far too much brandy and would nearly burn his eyebrows off.

250 g (8 oz) breadcrumbs

150 mL (¼ pint) milk

500 g (1 lb) raisins

250 g (8 oz) currants

250 g (8 oz) sultanas

150 g (5 oz) almonds, chopped

150 g (5 oz) mixed peel

juice and rind of 2 oranges and 1 lemon

2 teaspoons almond essence

2 teaspoons mixed spice

Brandy sauce

60 g (2 oz) butter

30 g (1 oz) plain flour

60 g (2 oz) cornflour

2 cups milk

2 tablespoons sugar

1 cup cream

3 tablespoons brandy

Mum made this fancy Christmas cake. You had to drizzle a spoonful of brandy over it every day. One Saturday night, Dad finished the bottle off. Mum was mortified. It was hospital brandy, first-aid for the cake.

Method

Chop the suet finely and mix it with the flour. Add the well-beaten eggs, sugar, and breadcrumbs. Add the milk, then the fruit, then the rest of the ingredients. Make sure it is well mixed. Cook it in a boiler or a pudding cloth for 4 hours before Christmas Day and allow another 2 hours on Christmas Day. Serve, flaming with brandy.

Make the sauce before lunch, and don't drink too much of the brandy. Melt the butter in a heavy saucepan. Blend in the plain flour, then the cornflour. Gradually add the milk and the sugar and bring to the boil. Stir continuously as it thickens. At the last moment add the cream and brandy and simmer gently. If the sauce is lumpy, beat with an egg whisk just before serving.

Mince pies

It will probably be New Year before you are in a fit state to eat these.

Ingredients

Pastry

1 cup plain flour

pinch salt

180 g (6 oz) butter or margarine

1 egg

1 heaped tablespoon sugar

Filling

1 cup sultanas

60 g (2 oz) mixed peel

½ cup currants

1 cup chopped raisins

½ cup raspberry jam

3 tablespoons sugar

grated rind and juice of 1 lemon

1 grated apple

Method

Sift flour and salt and rub in the margarine. Beat the egg with the sugar, add to the dry ingredients and mix to a dough. Wrap in greaseproof paper and leave in the refrigerator for 1 hour.

Prepare the filling by mixing fruits with jam, sugar, lemon rind and juice. Roll out half the pastry and line a tart plate. Put in filling. Roll out remaining pastry to fit the top. Trim the edges with a pinch or frill. Glaze with water, sprinkle with sugar and bake in a hot oven for 25 minutes. Serve while still warm with thick cream, or cold after Christmas dinner.

We always had fruit punch, full of passionfruit and bits of banana and lemonade. The only reason to drink it was that it always had a bottle of gin in it.

Be a Smart Cookie

Make this Old English Style Xmas Pudding with "Mother's Choice" FLOUR

Look for the Christmas recipes on every Mother's Choice Packet

AEROPHOS in Mother's Choice Flour is the *modern* raising ingredient

ENTOLETED the guaranteed way to ensure complete purity

ALWAYS FRESH the date of packing is stamped on every packet

VITAMIN ENRICHED Mother's Choice gives you extra vitamins for extra health!

Page 34

"Mother's Choice"
Old English Style Christmas Pudding
(Sufficient for two 2½-pint pudding basins)

COMBINE 1 lb. raisins, 4 ozs. sultanas, 4 ozs. currants, 4 ozs. chopped almonds, 4 ozs. chopped dates, 4 ozs. chopped prunes, 4 ozs. chopped cherries, 4 ozs. chopped peel.

POUR OVER ½ cup rum or sherry and allow to stand several hours.

CREAM 6 ozs. shortening and 8 ozs. brown sugar.

ADD 4 egg yolks—beating well after each addition.

MIX IN ½ cup marmalade.

SIFT TOGETHER 2 cups Mother's Choice Self-Raising Flour, 2 level teaspoons cinnamon, 1 level teaspoon nutmeg, ½ level teaspoon salt, ½ level teaspoon bi-carb. soda. Add 1 cup fine white breadcrumbs.

ADD ALTERNATELY the flour mixture and prepared fruit.

MIX IN ½ cup grated carrot, ½ cup grated apple, ½ cup hot milk, 1 tablespoon Parisienne essence.

FOLD IN 4 egg whites stiffly beaten.

PLACE in 2 greased pudding moulds and cover securely, or in a floured pudding cloth and tie with string.

STEAM OR BOIL 4 hours and further 2 hours on day of serving.

P.S.: If you want to cook the puddings one at a time, you can let the second stand while the first is steaming. Because Mother's Choice Self-Raising Flour contains "Aerophos," you can keep it for hours, if necessary, and the mixture won't lose a whit of its "rise-ability."

THE AUSTRALIAN WOMEN'S WEEKLY – December 4, 1957

COLD CHRISTMAS PUDDING

I was horrified when someone asked me to include this recipe. I was even more horrified when I looked at the ingredients. In fact, as long as you don't think it is *real* Christmas pudding, it's great.

Ingredients

900 mL (1½ pints) milk

3 tablespoons cocoa

3 dessertspoons gelatine

1 cup sugar

1 pinch salt

1 cup raisins

½ cup citrus peel

½ cup almonds, chopped

½ cup currants

½ cup dates

1 teaspoon vanilla

Method

Heat milk, cocoa and gelatine in a saucepan until the cocoa and gelatine are dissolved, but do not boil. Add sugar and salt, stir to dissolve them, and leave to cool. When the mixture begins to thicken, add the fruits, nuts and vanilla and pour into a mould. When set, turn out onto a plate. Pour over cold custard or whipped cream and put a sprig of holly on the top.

CHRISTMAS SHORTBREAD

Another one to save for the New Year.

Sixpences in the Christmas pudding. One year I broke a filling on mine, but I didn't care.

Ingredients

350 g (11 oz) plain flour

60 g (2 oz) ground rice

1 pinch salt

250 g (8 oz) butter

120 g (4 oz) caster sugar

We made the puddings at the beginning of November. Then they hung in their cloths in the cupboard until Christmas.

Method

Set oven at a low temperature and prepare a lightly greased tray. Mix the flour with the ground rice and salt. Cream the butter and sugar and then mix the flour into it (by hand) to make a dough. Divide the dough into four pieces, knead each one well, then roll each one out into an oval about 2 cm (⅔ in) thick. Prick with a fork and deckle the edges of the oval. Bake for about 30 minutes or until it is just browning. Cut into serving-size pieces while still hot.

I hated the food. Give us the presents and let us go.

CANDIED PEEL

For dedicated Christmas cooks and for children who are already bored with holidays.

Ingredients

4 orange rinds

4 lemon rinds

3 cups sugar

1½ cups water

salt

Method

Cut the rind into pieces and soak in slightly salted water for 2 days. Drain and rinse well. Boil in fresh water until

Atora is full of the nourishment of prime beef suet. Ready shredded, it saves you time and trouble.

Here's your **easy** recipe for

ATORA PUDDING WITH JAM

4-ozs. flour (with plain flour use 1 teaspoon baking powder). 2-ozs. sugar. 2-ozs. ATORA. 2 tablespoons milk. Pinch salt. 3 tablespoons jam.

Mix the dry ingredients together with milk. Put jam at bottom of greased basin. Put in the mixture (which must be stiff), and steam for 1½ hours.

HUGON'S

ATORA

SHREDDED BEEF SUET

the good BEEF SUET

HUGON & COMPANY LTD., MANCHESTER, II

We children were strictly forbidden to eat the cashews if we were offered the nuts. And we were only allowed a few muscatels. We could see Mum watching us as the bowl went round.

tender. Make a syrup with the sugar and 1½ cups of water. Boil for 5 minutes, allowing some evaporation. Put the rinds in the solution and leave for another 2 days. Boil them again for 20 minutes, then remove the rinds and lay them out on a biscuit tin. Put a little of the syrup in each piece of rind. Put into a very low oven for about 30 minutes to allow the rinds to dry.

We only ever got one Easter egg. Some kids made theirs last for ages. Mine was gone in a minute.

EASTER EGGS

If you are sick of having a glut of shop-bought chocolate Easter eggs, try these. Kids love making them.

At school, we made little baskets out of pink cardboard to put sweets in. We coloured in rabbits and stuck on cottonwool tails. And we prayed a lot.

Ingredients

30 g (1 oz) gelatine

1 L (1¾ pints) milk

120 g (4 oz) sugar

2 eggs

2 tablespoons grated chocolate

1 teaspoon vanilla

12 empty eggshells (as intact as possible)

Method

Soak the gelatine with a small amount of the milk for about 1 hour. Add to the rest of the milk and gradually bring to the boil, making sure the gelatine is dissolved. Stir in the sugar until completely dissolved.

Divide the mixture into two parts. Separate the eggs. To one half, add the grated chocolate. To the other, add the vanilla and the beaten yolks of the eggs. Heat, but do not boil.

Rinse out the eggshells (which must be pierced at one end first). Fill the shells with the mixtures. (There are plastic moulds you can buy as an easier alternative). You may prefer to mix them for a marbled effect or produce pure chocolate eggs or pure white eggs. Keep them upright by standing them in a tin with a layer of flour on the bottom. Allow to set for 24 hours. Break the shells carefully, arrange on red jelly and serve with icecream.

HOT CROSS BUNS

I know you can buy them at the supermarket, but there's nothing better than making your own.

Ingredients

500 g (1 lb) plain flour

1 pinch salt

20 g (⅔ oz) fresh yeast

60 g (2 oz) caster sugar

250 mL (8 fl oz) milk

60 g (2 oz) butter

120 g (4 oz) sultanas

2 eggs

2 teaspoons allspice

Method

Mix the flour and salt in a large ceramic basin. Put the yeast and 1 teaspoon of sugar in a cup and mix well. Warm the milk slightly, add the yeast mixture to it, and stir well. Make a dent in the centre of the flour and pour in the yeast and milk mixture. Mix into the flour, cover with a cloth and leave to rise in a warm place for 30 minutes. Knead gently on a floured board for 5 minutes. Return to the basin and gradually add the rest of the sugar, the milk, the butter, the sultanas, the eggs, and the allspice. Mix gently, but well.

Put a handful of the dough aside and add the spice to the remaining dough. Divide this into 12 equal pieces. Knead and place on a lightly greased biscuit slide. With the dough that was put aside, form a cross and press into the top of each bun. Put in a warm place and allow to rise for 20 minutes.

Set the oven at a high temperature. After 5 minutes, reduce the temperature to moderate and bake for another 10 minutes. Brush with a mixture of milk and beaten egg and return to the oven for another 5 minutes. (Total cooking time 20 minutes.)

I loved Easter. My sister had nightmares about the crucifixion. I only worried about the Easter Bunny.

Mum loved making the Easter buns. We always wished she'd buy them from the baker.

BIRTHDAY PARTIES

It was a set menu. Sausage rolls, frankfurts with toothpicks and little bowls of tomato sauce, sandwiches. That was the healthy part. Then we had cakes, fairy bread and chocolate crackles. The cakes were either butterfly cakes or little patty cakes with icing and those pearl decorations or chocolate sprinkles. There was orange cordial, and sometimes icecream and jelly. You didn't eat the birthday cake there. It was to take home in a piece of greaseproof paper.

My mother's cakes always came out lopsided. I remember the first time I persuaded her to buy one. Imagine! Real mock cream!

We used to have a plastic Mickey Mouse that went in the middle of all our birthday cakes. When I was ten, the heat of the candles got too much for him and he melted.

I threw up after every party. It never stopped me from eating my way through the next one.

We went to an enormous amount of trouble. Everyone had a hat. We made placecards. We had pink paper plates and there was a balloon for everyone. We sat down and in 30 seconds it was bedlam.

Mum cut up my birthday cake and wrapped up a slice for everyone to take home. There was none left for me. I have never forgiven her.

SECTION **J**

Kiddies' Party Tips!

Make a sparkling dessert from oranges halved (make fruit cup from the juice), scooped out, and filled with red jelly, topped with cream or Dairy Whip and sprinkled with hundreds and thousands.

Have a birthday cake decorated with the Christian names of all the little guests, and, of course, see that each one gets the slice with his or her name on it.

WHITE WINGS Self Raising FLOUR. Gives your baking that extra "lift"!

Gee, Mum! I could eat a million CHOCOLATE CRACKLES

The preparations were the most exciting. Writing out the invitations and giving them out at school. Buying the lollies. Making the cakes. I helped with all that, but Mum insisted on icing the cake. I didn't see it till the party. It had my name written on it. I couldn't believe it. It was like magic.

One girl had an icecream cake. I had to wait until my fortieth birthday.

I didn't like the food. I liked the gunfights.

Getting sent home from a party because I'd behaved badly was the most humiliating experience. I'd twirled round on their piano stool and knocked over a vase. I've never done it since.

Dad was the organiser of the games. We had paperchases and pin the tail on the donkey; treasure hunts and pass the parcel; oranges and lemons, blind man's bluff and musical chairs. The food was Mum's department. It was a bit of an anti-climax.

They don't make the hundreds and thousands the same now. They are a different shape and colour. I hate that.

9 LOLLIES

Making lollies is strictly for kids. When we baby boomer kids made them, we usually felt they weren't as good as the ones from the shops. Now, a touch of nostalgia and a wet Sunday afternoon may find you hunting for lolly recipes to help amuse your own children. Here are some sure-fire ones.

TOFFEE

We're all familiar with those home-made toffees. They used to come in paper patty pans and were sold to raise funds for dentists, the RSPCA and the Red Cross.

Ingredients

2 cups sugar

1 tablespoon golden syrup

1 dessertspoon butter

½ cup water

Method

Put sugar, golden syrup, butter and water into a saucepan. Heat very slowly until it comes to the boil. Continue to cook for another 5 minutes then pour into patty pans. Don't even think about eating them until they are cold, otherwise they will burn your mouth and rip your fillings out.

Those burnt toffees you made for stalls and sold for a penny.

give them
CONTENTMENT . . .
give them
CONFECTIONERY

I remember the feeling of pulling a toffee out of my mouth and realising there was a filling attached.

HONEYCOMB TOFFEE

This has the element of surprise and is more gratifying to make than plain old toffees.

Ingredients

1 cup sugar

2 tablespoons golden syrup

1 dessertspoon water

1 teaspoon bicarbonate soda

Method

Boil up sugar, golden syrup, and water. Keep on the boil for about 5 minutes. Take it off the stove and stir in a teaspoon of bicarbonate of soda. Pour out into a buttered cake tin and watch it fizz.

CARAMEL

If you keep sweetened condensed milk in your pantry, use it for caramel, not in the salad dressing.

Ingredients

120 g (4 oz) sugar

1 tin sweetened condensed milk

60 g (2 oz) butter

Method

Mix these ingredients and boil together on a low heat for 15 minutes, stirring constantly with a wooden spoon, bringing up the caramel from the bottom of the saucepan. The mixture will eventually turn a pale brown. Put in a shallow, buttered tin. When cold, cut into exactly equal squares.

CHOCOLATE FUDGE

Gluggy, sticky, gooey and deeply satisfying.

Ingredients

½ cup milk

2½ cups sugar

120 g (4 oz) butter

1 tablespoon cocoa

a few drops of vanilla essence

Method

Heat the milk and add the sugar, stirring until completely dissolved. Add the butter, the cocoa and the essence and cook for about 30 minutes on a gentle heat. Take off the stove and beat until the mixture thickens. Turn into a greased tray to set.

We'd make fudge about once a year—usually on a rainy winter afternoon. It was always a magic event.

Mum used to make coconut ice to take away on holidays. I think she did this so we wouldn't pester her for money. So there we'd be at the beach, with our coconut ice. It still seems strange not to have it.

COCONUT ICE

This is a rather more difficult recipe. It is important to get the mixture to the right consistency. This involves boiling it just long enough. It's worth the trouble. You may have been able to eat runny coconut ice as a child, but to an adult, it lacks appeal.

Ingredients

1 dessertspoon glucose

2 cups sugar

1 cup water

½ cup coconut

a few drops of cochineal

Method

Combine the glucose, sugar and water in a saucepan and stir continuously as you bring the mixture to the boil. Stop stirring once it comes to the boil and allow it to boil for 5 minutes. At this stage, test it by dropping a little of the mixture into cold water. If it is ready, it will form a soft ball. If it does not, it will have to be boiled a little longer. If the mixture is sticky, because it has been boiled too long, you will have to thin it with water and then boil it up again.

When you have determined that your coconut ice is ready, take it off the heat and allow it to stand a few minutes. Add the coconut and beat it until it is thick. Colour half the mixture with cochineal. Pour this half into a greased tin or bowl, then pour the other half over it. Allow to set, then cut into squares.

TURKISH DELIGHT

An exotic recipe from the Middle East, as reproduced in the *Presbyterian Women's Cookbook*.

Ingredients

30 g (1 oz) gelatine

CREAMY COCONUT ICE
(See recipe opposite page)

½ cup water

juice of 2 oranges

juice of 1 lemon

enough water to make the fruit juice up to 500 mL (16 fl oz)

500 g (1 lb) sugar

icing sugar and cornflour mixed together (about 4 parts icing
    sugar to 1 of cornflour)

Method

Soak the gelatine in the half cup of water. Put into a
saucepan with the fruit juice and the sugar. Heat until the
gelatine is dissolved. Pour into a wet tin. When set, cut
into squares and roll it in the icing sugar and cornflour
mixture.

WALNUT CREAMS

Baby boomers made these to impress the grownups. With any luck, the grownups didn't like them, or were at least gracious enough to share.

Ingredients

½ cup milk

2 cups sugar

a few drops of vanilla essence

120 g (4 oz) walnuts

Method

Combine the milk and sugar and bring to the boil in a heavy saucepan. Keep at a slow boil for 5 minutes. Add the vanilla and beat well. Form into small balls as the mixture cools. Press a walnut into each one. Allow to set in the refrigerator.

I loved lollies, mainly shop-bought ones like Violet Crumble and musk sticks. There's not a tooth in my head that hasn't been filled.

MARSHMALLOWS

If you like mucking round in the kitchen, licking out the bowl and creating something home-made, this recipe is for you. If you are into instant gratification, run immediately to the nearest milkbar.

Ingredients

20 g (¾ oz) gelatine

vanilla essence

12 tablespoons water

300 g (9½ oz) granulated sugar

1 dessertspoon glucose

1 egg white

Method

Combine the gelatine, the vanilla and half the water in a saucepan. Heat until the gelatine is dissolved. In a separate saucepan, boil the rest of the water with the sugar and the glucose. Combine the contents of the saucepans in a large bowl.

Beat the egg white until it is very stiff and fold it into the other ingredients. Whisk the mixture until it is thick and smooth. Turn into a tin which has been oiled and then dusted with icing sugar. Dust more icing sugar over the top of the mixture. Leave for 24 hours and then turn onto greaseproof paper which has been covered with icing sugar. Cut into squares, dredging each new side with icing sugar. Brush off the excess. Some people like it soft, but it is usually left for a day or two to harden before being eaten.

Two, four,
Touch the floor,
Six, eight,
Eating cherries off a plate.

Rocky road

This can be made with bought marshmallows or you can start from scratch and use the recipe above to make your own.

Ingredients

1 large block milk chocolate

1 packet marshmallows

a few glacé cherries, cut into quarters

1 small packet almonds, well chopped

Method

Melt the chocolate, chop up the marshmallows and arrange over the bottom of a small cake tin. Add some of the cherries and nuts and pour some of the chocolate over them. Add another layer of marshmallows, cherries and nuts and again fill up the holes with melted chocolate. Repeat until you run out of ingredients. Refrigerate. When set, cut into chunks.

Beth's frog in a bog

I felt extraordinarily jealous when Beth gave me this recipe. Okay, so it's not the sort of thing you serve at your dinner parties, but how come I never got it at *my* birthday parties? Guaranteed to please children and other imaginative people.

Ingredients

1 packet green jelly crystals

12 chocolate frogs

Method

Make up the green jelly using just a little less water than specified in the packet directions. Allow to cool. Just as it is beginning to set, pour about a quarter of it into a clear glass bowl. Put in 4 frogs. Pour more jelly on top of them

and add more frogs. Just keep going and then wait for it
to set.

Yes, you are allowed to use white frogs, snakes and
those lolly lizards. You're grown-up now and you can do
what you like.

Dishes for Invalids and Convalescents

Whenever I was sick my mother would grate up an apple and sprinkle it with sugar. I wish someone would do it these days.

Barley water was just so revolting. "The thicker the better," my mother used to say.

Beef tea was one thing. If you were really ill, you got raw beef tea, which was made by soaking mince meat in water. Then you drank the water. I felt sick just thinking about it.

My mother would say "He's off his food". I'd quake in terror thinking of the food she would feed me.

Beef tea custard. Need I say more.

Toast water was made by soaking toast in hot water and then straining it. I can't imagine what nutritional value it had.

Mum used to make me a little individual custard whenever I was sick. Yes, it made me feel better.

Invalid Cookery

Rules.
1. *Serve everything as daintily as possible.*
2. *The Doctor's orders must be strictly carried out.*
3. *Never serve the same mixture twice.*
4. *Do not study economy.*
5. *All food, hot or cold, should be sent from the kitchen, covered.*
6. *Do not leave food about in a sick room.*
7. *Serve a little food at a time and serve it often.*

Beverages.
1. *Nourishing as milk, barley water.*
2. *Medicinal, as rice water, toast water.*
3. *Thirst-quenching, as lemonade.*

Diets.
1. *Ordinary or full diet consists of meat, vegetables and pudding.*
2. *Low Diet—liquids, such as beef tea.*
3. *Milk diet—milk, sago, rice, etc.*
4. *Vegetable diet, only white meats and vegetables are allowed.*
5. *Meat diet, only meat dishes and cheese, eggs, broths, etc., are allowed.*

We had a funny thing of having sweet milk thickened with cornflour. It sounds revolting, but it was quite comforting.

I had brains every day I had the measles. Doctor's orders. I've never had them since.

We had hot honey and lemon drinks for a cold. They were wonderful.

Lemon jelly was the only sort you were allowed when you were sick. As you were getting better, you had a spoonful of custard on it.

10 BABY BOOMER RECIPES BEST FORGOTTEN

Everybody hates me, nobody loves me,
I'm going to go and eat worms.
Big fat juicy ones,
Itsey bitsey teeny ones,
I'm going to eat some worms.

When researching, writing and talking about baby boomer food, I have often felt a twinge of guilt for poking fun at it. After all, my poor mum slaved over a hot stove along with the rest of her generation, turning out cooked breakfasts, packed lunches, morning and afternoon teas, baked dinners, stews, mixed grills, casseroles and hot and cold puds of infinite variety. Today, we've rejected the "food is love" philosophy of that era and enjoy a more relaxed attitude to food. We also, on the whole, enjoy better food.

This book is a celebration of great baby boomer food. But I still can't resist having a look at some of the shockers I came across in my research. *Stewed fish, sheep's head fricassee* and *sausages in batter* are self-explanatory. (There was an awful lot of stewing—*stewed kidney, stewed neck chops, stewed pigeons, stewed sweetbreads* and *stewed tongue.*) But there were other recipes which required further investigation.

What, for instance, were *Ammonia biscuits?* Biscuits with a teaspoon of ammonia. All you ammonia sniffers out there might like to try it. Maybe in the stew or a roast too.

I blanched at the recipe for *Ox eyes*, but my fascination with horror recipes made me read on. It turned out to be poached eggs on slices of tomato. I doubt the name did much to add to its popularity. Likewise *Toad-in-a-hole.* These are sausages baked in flour and water. They sound as bad as the name implies.

There were some other ghastly names. *Bloater paste* turns out to be a fairly innocuous fish paste. *Convent mould* was a fancy jelly from a Catholic cookbook.

Isn't it gorgeous?

The polka dot cake you make so easily... with Puffin Cake Mix!

"There's nothing more popular than layer cake, and this one is made specially delicious and gay with colourful chocolate buttons!" says *Betty King*

Home Economist of World Brands

This is the kind of cake you'll be so proud to bring in . . . a high-rising, light, rich-flavoured layer cake with a fine, moist texture that stays fresh and delicious to the very last slice. Marvellous to think you make this beauty with no effort at all — with Puffin Cake Mix!

From packet to oven in next to no time!
It takes mere minutes to work this kind of cake-making magic. You merely add eggs and milk to Puffin Cake Mix. No weighing, no creaming or tiring beating — and only one bowl needed.
You mix and bake according to the simple directions for layer-cakes given on the Puffin packet. When baked, sandwich the layers with your favourite icing (try one of the recipes on the Puffin packet) and frost all over with the same creamy icing. Now take the little chocolate buttons (we've used Cadbury's Dairy Milk Rolls) and press all over. Wasn't that quick?

Special ingredients in Puffin guarantee success
You just can't have a flop with Puffin, because Puffin contains specially milled flour, enriched shortening, cane sugar and top-quality raising ingredients, all blended more smoothly and accurately than you could ever do at home. Success is guaranteed — a gorgeous cake, or double your money back.

How about Polka Dot cake for a surprise tonight?

Golden! Light!

Scones more delicious than ever before with New Puffin Scone Mix!

Just add milk to new Puffin Scone Mix — then mix and bake. Fifteen minutes later you're looking at the highest, lightest, most handsome scones you've ever baked! *No more weighing, sifting, measuring or rubbing in the shortening.*

All the work — gone forever! Puffin Scones are made with such little effort, you'll never stop being amazed.

Puffin Scone Mix makes many other delicious recipes, too.
Pikelets, pancakes, rock cakes, savoury pinwheels and tea-cakes . . . they're but a few of the delicious variety of recipes you'll make so easily and quickly with Puffin Scone Mix. All the recipes are right on the Puffin packet.

Double-money-back guarantee
— so try Puffin soon as you like.

Some of the names of recipes reflect the failure of the imagination in that era. Who thought up *Bruce's biscuits?* Bruce, I suppose, but was that all he could rise to? At least it was better than *Nice plain biscuits. Boiled sausages* is nothing if not descriptive. *Quince jelly (unfailing)* seems to indicate a certain level of desperation and *Paradise pudding without eggs* is definitely giving itself airs.

There was a certain coyness in some of the recipes. Vegetables came dressed and *masking sauce* is a constant theme. Nobody explains what exactly it was supposed to mask. Maybe *Boiled sheep's tongue.*

Some of the recipes took up the challenge of haute cuisine. Generally, like *Carpet bag à la Wagga Wagga* or *Indian fritters*, the reality fell a little short. The Indian theme, via a tin of curry powder on the pantry shelf, was constant in our lives. Sick of rabbit pie? Try *curried rabbit and rice, curried brains*, or the one we all remember— *minced roast curry.*

In their search for variety and their need for economy, our mothers were lured into some strange culinary territory. *Mock duck* was a strange way of cooking lamb. *Pickled steak* was a way of doing the steak when it had, well, gone off a bit. *Tongue and chestnuts* was obviously designed to stop them saying, "We don't like tongue". *Ginger chokoes* was a last ditch attempt to use up the chokoes that just wouldn't stop growing over the outside dunny.

The recipes of the era reflect the cooking methods. Stewing was a time-honoured method. Try *Stewed barracouta in milk.* If sausages could be boiled, so could anything. Tripe was fried along with scones and brains. Fricassee was just stew to you and me, and devilling meant a dash of pepper. If you wanted to make your fricassee of neck chops really fancy, you added a masking sauce.

I'd always thought custard was something you served with dessert. Thank goodness my mother never made *Cornflakes custard* or, even worse, *savoury custard.*

Eating everything up and leaving a clean plate was the sign of a good child. But sometimes, as the above recipes show, well, we just couldn't be good.

BABY BOOMER RECIPES BEST FORGOTTEN

Ammonia biscuits
Barracouta in milla
Bloater paste
Convent mould
Curried brains
Dressed vegetables
Fricassee of neck chops
    with white sauce
Fried tripe
Ginger chokoes
Lamb's fry
Mutton and mushroom
    pudding
Pickled steak
Raw beef tea
Sausages in batter
Savoury custard
Sheep's head broth
Sheep's head fricassee
Stewed sweetbread
Stewed tripe and onion
Toad-in-a-hole
Toast water
Tongue and chestnuts

MAYONNAISE MIXED TO YOUR OWN TASTE
IN TWO MINUTES WITH
NESTLÉ'S MILK

**JUST USE
NESTLÉ'S MILK
KEEN'S MUSTARD AND
SEPPELTS VINEGAR
...MIX AND STIR
...THAT'S ALL!**

All you need: ¼ tin Nestlé's Sweetened Condensed Milk; ½ teaspoon salt; ¼ cup Seppelts Vinegar; 1 teaspoon Keen's Mustard. Mix all the ingredients thoroughly and stir until mixture thickens.

Allow to stand for a few minutes to stiffen, then test for your individual taste. Unlike factory-made mayonnaise you can vary it to your own taste as much as you like. Deliciously different!

21

IT'S MARVELLOUS WHAT YOU CAN DO WITH NESTLÉ'S MILK !
Remember, it's milk and sugar all in one – perfect for "creaming" Nescafé, Ricory, cocoa or tea.

NM.132.FPC.

Storing Health for the Years ahead

CORNWELL'S
EXTRACT
OF MALT

A REAL FOOD

CORNWELL'S
Extract of MALT

A PURE TONIC FOOD FOR BUILDING STURDY BODIE

ACKNOWLEDGEMENTS

The publishers have made every effort to contact the copyright holders of all material included in *The Baby Boomers' Cookbook*. They would be pleased to hear from anyone who has not been duly acknowledged.

Simon & Schuster and Helen Townsend would like to thank the following for their kind permission to reproduce illustrative material.

Arnott's Biscuits Limited (pp. 125, 134, 145)
Australian Wine and Brandy Corporation (p. 181)
Banana Growers' Federation (p. 100)
Bushell's Tea and Coffee (p. 131)
Campbell's Australasia (front cover — Campbell's Tomato Juice can)
Cerebos (Australia) Ltd (p. 174)
Clive of India (p. 83)
Collins/Angus & Robertson Publishers for the illustration and legend from *The Commonsense Cookery Book* © NSW Cookery Teachers' Association 1970, 1974, 1988 (p. 10)
Corning Australia (p. 15)
CSR Wood Panels (main cover illustration)
Davis Gelatine (Aust) (pp. 57, 161)
Email Ltd (pp. 5, 37)
EOI Pty Limited for the illustrations from *Betty King's Cookbook* (pp. vi, 48, 116, 121, 141, 148, 165) and the Copha Vegetable Shortening advertisement (p. 66)
G.E.C. Australia Ltd incorporated in NSW (p. 79)
H J Heinz Co Aust Ltd (p. 185)
Kraft Foods Limited (front cover — Vegemite and Kraft Cheddar, pp. 68, 81, 84, 93)
Kellogg (Aust) Pty Ltd (pp. 69, 128)
L & K: Rexona Pty Ltd (p. 95)
Mauri Grocery Pty Ltd (p. 178)
McWilliams Wines (p. 60)

Meadow Lea Foods (pp. 25, 129)
Mobil Oil Australia Ltd (p. 59)
Nestle Aust Ltd (pp. 73, 177)
Peters Ice Cream (p. 56)
Sabco Ltd (p. 89)
Samuel Taylor (pp. 12, 69, 88, 169, 170)
Shawsno Pty Ltd trading as Henry Jones Foods
    (p. 108)
Sunbeam Victa Corporation (pp. 4, 29, 35, 137)
Taubmans Pty Ltd (p. 4)
Traders Pty Limited, from the archives of the
    Aeroplane Jelly Company, 8 Wharf Road, West
    Ryde (pp. 16, 62, 64, 171)
Unifoods Pty Ltd (pp. 71, 77, 90, 113)
Weldon Publishing and Pembroke School for the
    illustrations and text from *Green and Gold
    Cookbook*, 44th edition, Weldon Publishing, 1991
    (pp. v, 23, 41, 106, 144)
White Wings Foods (recipe cards pp. 76, 86, 87, 93,
    96, 120, 121, 158 and pp. 40, 53, 65, 151, 173)

RECIPE INDEX

WEIGHTS AND MEASURES

The number of tablespoons to 30 grams (1 ounce)

Breadcrumbs, dry	3
Breadcrumbs, fresh	5
Cheese, grated	4
Cocoa	4
Cornflour	3
Flour, unsifted	3
Gelatine, granulated	3
Golden syrup	1
Jam	1
Margarine	2
Oatmeal	2
Rolled oats	4
Treacle	1

Weight of a level cup in grams (ounces)

Bacon, chopped	150 g (5 oz)
Breadcrumbs, dry	180 g (6 oz)
Breadcrumbs, fresh	90 g (3 oz)
Cabbage, raw, shredded	60 g (2 oz)
Carrots, diced	180g (6 oz)
Cheese, grated	120 g (4 oz)
Cocoa	120 g (4 oz)
Cornflour	150 g (5 oz)
Flour, unsifted	160 g (5½ oz)
Golden syrup	480 g (16 oz)
Lentils	270 g (9 oz)
Margarine	240 g (8 oz)
Minced beef	240 g (8 oz)
Oatmeal	210 g (7 oz)
Peas	270 g (9 oz)
Potato, mashed	240 g (8 oz)
Raisins	210 g (7 oz)
Rolled oats	120 g (4 oz)
Semolina	210 g (7 oz)
Sugar (white)	240 g (8 oz)
Sultanas	240 g (8 oz)
Treacle	480 g (16 oz)